Using Video to Assess Teaching Performance

Using Video to Assess Teaching Performance

A Resource Guide for edTPA

EDITED BY
CARRIE EUNYOUNG HONG, PH.D.
IRENE VAN RIPER, ED.D.

ROWMAN & LITTLEFIELD
Lanham • Boulder • New York • London

Published by Rowman & Littlefield
A wholly owned subsidiary of The Rowman & Littlefield Publishing Group, Inc.
4501 Forbes Boulevard, Suite 200, Lanham, Maryland 20706
www.rowman.com

Unit A, Whitacre Mews, 26-34 Stannary Street, London SE11 4AB

British Library Cataloguing in Publication Information Available

Library of Congress Cataloging-in-Publication Data is Available

ISBN 978-1-4758-3218-1 (cloth: alk. paper)
ISBN 978-1-4758-3219-8 (pbk: alk. paper)
ISBN 978-1-4758-3220-4 (electronic)

∞™ The paper used in this publication meets the minimum requirements of
American National Standard for Information Sciences—Permanence of Paper for
Printed Library Materials, ANSI/NISO Z39.48-1992.

Printed in the United States of America

This book is dedicated to all P-12 teachers who make a difference in the lives of children. Behind every successful person is a great teacher. Thank you for your commitment to improve education and strengthen the teaching profession.

I dedicate this book to my family and friends who have inspired me to continue my ongoing journey of growth as a teacher educator. To my husband and daughter, thank you for your unwavering support and encouragement.

—C. E. H.

This book is dedicated to my husband who has provided me with sustained support and encouragement throughout my career and for offering his expertise in editing to help make this book a reality. Also, to my son and his family who inspire me with love and laughter, thank you.

I dedicate this book to all the passionate teachers who enter the classroom every day, bringing excellence to each and every student.

—I. V. R.

Contents

Preface

The educational climate in the US has been increasingly interested in accountability, with a succession of governmental mandates for testing and evaluation of both students and teachers. Now, many states have adopted the certification standards of edTPA, a performance-based assessment process that strives to ensure that new teachers are "ready for the job." It is no surprise that video recordings of teacher candidates in the classroom are a required part of the process.

This is the reason we, as teachers have, written this book. It is intended to be a resource manual for teacher candidates building an edTPA portfolio, or any teacher who is interested in improving their pedagogy through the use of self-recorded classroom videos. Imagine a group of teachers, from "old pros" to fledgling "newbies," sharing video clips over tea and coffee. A teacher is never too old to learn something new, or too young to have a good idea.

But don't just go to school tomorrow and prop your smartphone up on a spare desk! There are many considerations to take into account before you start recording; some technical and some legal. We hope we have addressed them all clearly and completely in this book, but if you have any questions or concerns, we strongly advise that you ask for help from your instructors or administrators before hitting the "Record" button.

From the beginning, technology in education has focused on ways to better inform the student. A slab of slate and a piece of chalk has evolved through whiteboards and erasable felt tip markers, electronic smart boards and beyond, in ever-improving means of displaying a lesson. But what about technological improvements to help a teacher be better at teaching?

Enter the advent of classroom video recording. With the increasingly ubiquitous presence of easily operated and relatively inexpensive video recording apparatus, such as smart phones, teachers are now able to observe themselves, as well as others, in order to assess the pros and cons of pedagogical techniques.

Reviewing one's own classroom video often results in comments such as; "Do I really do that all the time?", and, "Why didn't I get them engaged in more discussion?" Being freed from the mental focus on the lesson of the moment, a teacher can see a more complete picture of their performance. It then becomes easier to find areas for improvement.

Video has great potential to enrich the art and science of teaching. Video technology is a useful tool for both beginning and experienced teachers to reflect on their instruction to support students' engagement in learning. Teachers can benefit from an analysis of classroom interactions by making changes in their instructional strategies to deepen student learning.

Acknowledgments

We would like to thank the chapter authors for their invaluable contributions. We are grateful for their exemplary work and their passion to improve teacher education. This book could not have been written without their professional expertise.

We are deeply indebted to Joe Van Riper who helped us edit and format this work. We are grateful for his technical expertise and his strong support.

Finally, we acknowledge the fine support from the team at Rowman & Littlefield.

Introduction

Preparing teachers to use a range of educational technology is a vital curricular topic in teacher education. Among many technologies, the importance of video should not be overlooked. Despite its positive benefits to improve teacher instruction and student performance, there has been a dearth of awareness and training to help teachers effectively utilize video recordings of authentic teaching for professional development and growth.

This volume is developed to offer conceptual frameworks, strategies, and practical suggestions in preparing teacher candidates to take advantage of video-based reflection and analysis during clinical practice. Specifically, this book offers a resource guide in the process of edTPA.

edTPA is a performance-based teacher assessment developed by the Stanford Center for Assessment, Learning and Equity. As a nationally available standards-based assessment, teacher education institutions in many states have adopted edTPA to assess teacher candidates' readiness to teach. edTPA is a subject-specific assessment and reviews a teacher candidate's authentic teaching to support student learning in different teaching fields.

This book is divided into four chapters. Chapter 1 reviews current research on the use of video in teacher education and provides a strategic framework for effective video analysis. Using the suggested questionnaire, readers can determine their level of background knowledge and understanding of video analysis as a teaching and learning tool. The chapter emphasizes systemic and contextualized methods of video analysis in teacher education, underscoring the need for experienced guidance.

Chapter 2 provides readers with a detailed guide on the use of video footage in the creation of a high-quality edTPA portfolio. The chapter discusses the importance of video evidence as a central component of an edTPA portfolio with attention to relevant edTPA tasks and rubrics. Using the information provided in this chapter, teacher candidates can improve analytic skills of instructional practice.

Chapter 3 focuses on collaborative strategies for successful edTPA assessment. For the intended audience of teacher candidates, cooperating teachers, and field supervisors or mentors, the chapter promotes collaborative efforts that lead to the effective use of video analysis in the process of preparing and submitting edTPA portfolios. The chapter also provides reference materials to assist the target audience.

Chapter 4 provides an overview of technologies that teacher candidates can utilize for video recording. The chapter walks through a step-by-step guidance for creating an authentic teaching video. Concrete tips with a checklist and a flowchart will be helpful for teacher candidates who prepare for their own edTPA submission.

Video Analysis in Teacher Education: Overview and Framework

CARRIE EUNYOUNG HONG
AND IRENE VAN RIPER

Today's teachers and students live in a technologically advanced world. Among these new technologies, the use of authentic teaching video is not a new idea in education. Although video viewing and analysis has a long history with extensive research and scholarly review, use of video in teacher education has been rejuvenated along with recent educational reform efforts, such as performance-based assessments for teacher certification.

This chapter provides readers with an overview of video analysis in teacher preparation by reviewing current research on video-based analysis to enhance teacher candidates' knowledge and skills. Research-based strategies for effective use of video in teacher education courses and an evidence-based analysis of teacher practice will be explored. The target audience of this chapter includes, but is not limited to, teacher educators, teacher candidates, field supervisors, and cooperating teachers.

VIDEO TECHNOLOGY REDEFINES TEACHER EDUCATION

Over the past few decades, researchers have documented a great deal about how video can support teacher candidates' learning of effective teaching and assist them in honing their instructional skills. Although the use of video has not been considered as a significant curricular requirement for initial teacher preparation, yet its significance and benefits are increasingly recognized by researchers and teacher educators alike. Video-based analysis of teacher practice has become popular over the past 10 years in teacher education programs for a wide range of subject areas, at all grade levels, and around the world (Gaudin & Charliès, 2015).

In the United States, video-based reflection of teaching practice has been recommended as a means of institutional reforms for states that have adopted performance-based assessments, such as edTPA (Educator Teacher Preparation Assessment). As an educative assessment, edTPA requires candidates to provide authentic evidence of their teaching by submitting recorded video clips in which candidates demonstrate how they support and engage students in content-specific learning (Stanford Center for Assessment, Learning and Equity, 2017). Specifically, candidates reflect on various aspects of their instruction by referring to scenes and examples from the video clips of their clinical practice.

The rapidly growing use of video in teacher education is partially due to technology advances. The equipment needed for recording teacher instruction can easily be found at hand. Moreover, transferring or sharing video clips with other teachers has become much easier with modern high-speed Internet access. For example, most teacher candidates are familiar with using digital cameras or other video-recording devices to capture their real-time teaching.

Electronic files of recorded video can be stored on one's cell phone and, if needed, be transferred easily to different devices. Most recently, video files can be uploaded to Internet-based data storage or web servers, and be downloaded to any device anytime and anywhere. In addition, a video editing software with an extensive range of features allows one to edit video for various purposes to a broad audience of teachers.

In the near future, a variety of advanced tools will be available for digital annotation, which allows more sophisticated video analysis of instructional practice. Consequently, advances in video technology afford novice teachers even greater access to authentic classroom events than other traditional methods of classroom observation, which require one's physical presence in a classroom.

In relevant literature, various terms are used to describe similar ideas and concepts. The most frequently used terms in the current field of research are video recording, video viewing, video watching, video analysis, video-based reflection, video annotation, video clubs, and so on. For consistency, we will use the phrase "video viewing" to refer to an activity in which candidates watch recorded video of authentic teaching.

Video analysis means a series of activities that candidates do with the video they watched. For example, while watching a video, candidates may identify classroom events, activities or behaviors; interpret what has been observed from the video; and analyze what they have noticed in order to improve their knowledge and skills. During video analysis, candidates may write commentary, respond to given prompts, discuss their thoughts with others, or provide feedback on student performance.

Most research in video analysis underlines that the objectives of video-based teacher education must target improving candidates' professional abilities to teach in a real classroom. Also, the learning goals of video analysis must be aligned to promote teacher changes and growth (Tripp & Rich, 2012). Literature has identified two main objectives to achieve when video is used in teacher education. The primary objectives are

1. to expose teacher candidates to a wide variety of professional practices (Newhouse, Lane, & Brown, 2007; Seidel, Blomberg, & Renkl, 2013) and
2. to stimulate candidates' professional reflection (Coffey, 2014; McCullagh, Bell, & Corscadden, 2013; Santagata & Angelici, 2010; Sherin & van Es, 2009).

Yet, one may argue that video cannot replace the required hours of field experience and physical observations of classroom teaching that teacher candidates must fulfill before student teaching or clinical practice. It is essential that candidates acquire content-specific knowledge and pedagogical skills before they practice their instruction with school-age students. For this reason, most teacher preparation programs require candidates to observe authentic classroom teaching performed by experienced teachers in various school settings and to actively engage in interacting with students with special needs and diverse learners.

We would like to caution readers that simply watching video clips of classroom instruction does not make a difference in learning and teaching. Video is a tool as well as a medium. Its benefits are defined by the way it is used. Therefore, a critical review of video analysis, its effective design and implementation in teacher preparation programs, and its effects on instruction and student learning must be incorporated in order to warrant its success in teacher training. We hope this chapter serves as a springboard for collaborative actions and reform efforts in video-based teacher education.

Before moving on to the next section, we recommend that candidates review the following questions as a way to evaluate their background knowledge about video analysis.

- Have you observed any kinds of authentic classroom teaching by watching recorded video clips? In what circumstances did you watch them? What was the intended purpose?
- Have you ever been trained in watching a classroom video of your own or another teacher's?
- What would you do while watching video clips of classroom teaching? What kinds of things would you pay attention to?
- Why would you watch recorded teaching of your own or other teachers? What do you expect to take away from this activity?
- Do you know how to identify specific events in a video clip or to analyze what is going on in the video?

- As a result of video analysis, what do you expect to learn so that you become a better teacher?

If you are a teacher candidate, how many questions were you able to answer? Which question(s) did you find difficult to answer? It is not surprising if you are ill-prepared to view and analyze video of classroom teaching by other teachers, not to mention viewing and analyzing video clips of your own teaching. Up until now, video analysis has not been a mandatory curricular topic in most teacher preparation programs of the United States. Partially due to recent requirements of performance-based assessments, video analysis received significant attention as an important skill that candidates must be aware of and be trained to perform effectively.

If you are a teacher educator and interested in using video analysis with candidates, you can utilize these questions as a pre-assessment tool to know about candidates' prior training and background knowledge. Your students may or may not have sufficient background knowledge or experience in video analysis. Checking candidates' readiness for video analysis helps you determine to what extent your scaffolding and guidance are needed.

Once you have the candidates' answers to these questions, reflect on what you learned about your students' readiness to participate in video-based analysis of teaching practice. Research shows that with careful planning and professional guidance, video analysis can evolve as a routine and familiar professional practice in teacher education programs (Baecher & Kung, 2011).

Moreover, many teacher educators agree that video-based reflection is a critical assessment tool through which candidates can demonstrate their content knowledge and instructional skills (Wiens, Hessberg, LoCasale-Crouch, & DeCoster, 2013). In the following section, we will provide readers with an overview of video analysis in teacher education, its benefits and limitations.

VIDEO ANALYSIS IN TEACHER EDUCATION

Research on video analysis in teacher education has reported that teacher candidates benefit from viewing and analyzing authentic video of classroom teaching. It is essential that the use of video is well structured with clear objectives and explicit guidance by experts (Baecher & Tuten, 2011; Marsh, Mitchell, & Adamczyk, 2009).

Video can be effective in creating a learning environment in which candidates actively construct knowledge and interact with others (Koc, Peker, & Osmanoglu, 2009). Video is an effective training tool as it provides a common ground for candidates and teacher educators to explore and discuss various issues of teaching practice.

Similarly, video can be useful to engage candidates in problem solving and decision-making for effective instruction. Analyzing concrete issues observed in the video is cognitively more challenging than dealing with hypothetical scenarios about classroom teaching. In other words, video provides an authentic context of teaching and learning through which candidates can be immersed into a complex interplay of teacher instruction and student performance and a myriad of educational issues that beginning teachers should be aware of.

Benefits of Video Analysis

Many researchers and teacher educators agree that video can be a valuable tool in educating teacher candidates for a range of educational topics and training them to perform a wide range of instructional practices.

A number of empirical studies have documented that teacher candidates improved their learning and teaching from a well-conceptualized video analysis embedded in education courses (e.g., Arya, Christ, & Chiu, 2014; Coffey, 2014; Marsh, Mitchell, & Adamczyk, 2009; Welsch & Devlin, 2007). Most of these studies highlight that the benefits and potential of video analysis for preservice teachers can be maximized when its implementation has a clear purpose and is well structured.

Blomberg, Sherin, Renkl, Glogger, and Seidel (2014) illustrate several benefits when video of authentic teaching is effectively used to prepare teacher candidates:

1. Video serves to link theory with practice, so candidates can acquire theoretical knowledge by observing ways theory is applied in real classroom settings.
2. Video is a learning tool by which teacher candidates can practice applying their theoretical knowledge to make sense of classroom practice.
3. Video offers a wide range of teaching practices as a secondhand experience of instruction, so candidates can enhance their pedagogical knowledge.

Based on reviews of relevant studies on the use of video in teacher education, Tripp and Rich (2012) summarized the benefits of video reflection as follows:

> Teachers were able to (a) identify gaps between their beliefs about good teaching and their actual teaching practices, (b) articulate their tacit assumptions and purposes about teaching and learning, (c) notice things about their teaching that they did not remember, (d) focus their reflections on multiple aspects of classroom teaching, and (e) assess the strengths and weaknesses of their teaching.
>
> (p. 729)

An empirical study of video analysis documented to what extent video helps teacher candidates reflect on their teaching (Rosaen, Lundeberg, Cooper, Fritzen, & Terpstra, 2010). Using a case study method, Rosaen et al. (2010) examined ways candidates reflected on their lessons during their student teaching by engaging in memory-based and video-based methods of reflection. The candidates' written commentary when they reflect on their student teaching from video was compared with their commentary when they reflect from memory.

The researchers found that the candidates (a) wrote more specific comments about their teaching from video reflection than writing from memory, (b) shifted their attention from classroom management in memory-based reflection to instruction in video-based reflection, and (c) paid more attention to the children when they reflected on video clips (p. 348).

Other studies also reported significant changes and growth in ways teacher candidates reflect on their own and peers' teaching practice (see Baecher & Tuten, 2011; Harford, MacRuairc, & McCartan, 2010; Newhouse, Lane, & Brown, 2007; Tripp & Rich, 2012). For example, Harford et al.'s (2010) study examined the effects of peer video analysis in which teacher candidates analyzed each other's video and reflected on their instruction.

Harford et al. concluded, "This [peer video analysis] fostered the construct of self-education and located the ownership of the process firmly within the student teacher group" (p. 65). If used in a collaborative setting, video analysis can serve as a learning tool among teacher candidates.

Meanwhile, Fadde and Sullivan (2013) used an interactive video method using the *expert-novice research* paradigm. In their research, experienced teacher educators and teacher candidates viewed the same video clips. Teacher educators' (experts) observations of the video clip were shared with teacher candidates (novices) on how to notice classroom events as experts would do. Then, teacher candidates wrote their observations of given topics (i.e., classroom management, student questioning) to compare them with those of the experts.

When carefully planned and supported, the interactive nature of video analysis benefits candidates in constructing their knowledge and reflecting on their practice. The interactive video method within the expert–novice framework allows candidates to receive expert feedback on specific issues (Santagata & Angelici, 2010). With experienced educators' scaffolding and professional feedback, candidates have an opportunity to correct their misconceptions or misunderstanding of teaching practice as well as to refine their pedagogical knowledge.

Similarly, a range of research studies have documented that using video in a content-focused methods course is an effective way to enhance candidates' learning as it helps engage candidates in an in-depth analysis in which a single video clip can be analyzed multiple times from multiple lenses (Welsch & Devlin, 2007).

For example, during the first time of watching a video clip, candidates may focus their attention on specific content issues. Then, they can shift their attention to classroom management or instructional issues when they watch the same clip a second time. Refined integration of video analysis with specific pedagogical strategies can encourage candidates to use higher-order thinking and interpret classroom events and behaviors from multiple perspectives (Brunvand, 2010; Rosaen, Lundeberg, Cooper, Fritzen, & Terpstra 2008).

Limitations of Video

The use of video in teacher education still has many limitations. First, technical issues may prevent effective use of video in teacher education courses. Video can fail to capture some aspects of classroom activities, such as group interaction or nonverbal behaviors off-camera. Considering that video is a snapshot of a reality that is based on the focus and the angle of the camera, information captured and recorded is more limited than what would have been seen by an observer in the classroom.

Other limitations also exist when candidates participate in video-based activities. The objective of video analysis should not be focused on characterizing good and bad teaching practices. Using video of other teachers' instruction to determine good versus bad practices raises serious ethical issues.

On the other hand, video should not be used to determine only exemplary lessons. Teacher candidates can develop analytic skills even from ill-prepared or mediocre lessons. Others warn that candidates should not simply provide a list of events and behaviors observed in the classroom video. This kind of surface-level analysis leads to a false impression of teacher reflection.

Video analysis can be implemented and practiced in any teacher education courses. Examining effective practices of video analysis, researchers highlighted that methods of video analysis may vary, depending on content areas. It is difficult to generalize effective methods that would work for diverse purposes. The learning objectives of video analysis must determine which instructional strategy should be selected to train teacher candidates (Blomberg et al., 2014; Seidel, Blomberg, & Renkl, 2013).

Research also reports the resistance of teacher education faculty and cooperating teachers regarding the use of video for analyzing candidates' lesson. If contextual information is not provided or is insufficient, a full understanding of the instruction has limits.

Most of all, there is a general consensus among researchers and teacher educators, who value the benefits of video. That is, analysis of classroom video should not replace real-time observation or authentic interaction with students. To avoid this, teacher educators must emphasize that video is a supplementary tool to acquire professional knowledge and skills.

CONCEPTUAL FRAMEWORK FOR EFFECTIVE VIDEO ANALYSIS

Video can reach its full potential when it is used with clear objectives and goals. There is no doubt that teacher candidates need explicit support and planned guidance to draw their attention to certain classroom events or behaviors.

This support can be provided as a form of guided video analysis that includes a range of scaffolded learning activities for candidates to engage in. These activities can be expert scaffolding, directed prompts for focused attention, collaborative discussion, expert commentary, guidance for an in-depth analysis, guided reflection, a series of checklists, or observation protocol.

How did guided video analysis work to improve candidates' knowledge and skills? Research has identified two critical components of the guided video analysis that make it effective to enhance teacher knowledge and practice (van Es, 2010). First, roles of facilitators who have professional knowledge and extensive experience are crucial to improving teacher learning during video analysis. Second, the selection of appropriate video clips to meet learning goals of video-based reflection affects the success of these activities.

Research also shows that experienced teachers are able to describe classroom events by rationalizing why they occur, for what purposes, whereas beginning teachers tend to simply describe what they observe (Berliner, 1986; Maclean & White, 2007). Noticeable differences between experienced teachers and novice teachers during video-based reflection are related to ways they make connections of observable behaviors with broad instructional contexts.

Blomberg et al. (2014) identified three levels of difference between experienced and novice teachers when they reflected on their own recorded teaching: description, evaluation, and integration (p. 445).

Description means that one is able to identity what has been observed or to differentiate among classroom events and behaviors without making any professional judgments. *Evaluation* refers to one's ability to reflect on what has been observed in a context of objectives of the lesson and student learning outcomes. Finally, *integration* is described as one's ability to link classroom events to one's conceptual understanding of teaching and learning. During the phase of integration in particular, teachers with years of experience are capable of classifying what has been analyzed into a broad frame of teaching and learning contexts.

This framework of description, evaluation, and integration addresses a continuum of a teacher's professional abilities as a growth model (see figure 1.1). If we apply this framework to teacher training, growth of teacher performance is expected to occur in the continuum of novices to experts.

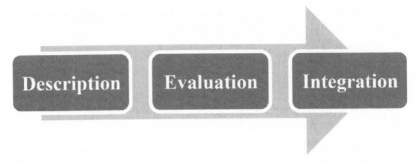

FIGURE 1.1
Professional abilities of video-based reflection from novices to experienced teachers
Source: Carrie Eunyoung Hong

For example, when watching a video clip of their own teaching for the first time, novice teachers may be able to describe a series of classroom events that take place in the clip with experts' guidance or without any assistance. Then, with practice, they identify or differentiate among various events and behaviors, but may not be able to evaluate their instruction, such as what they should not have done or what they should have done differently.

With experience and practice, novice teachers begin to evaluate their instruction by reflecting on their teaching and student learning with clear alignment to specific learning goals. Finally, novice teachers become experienced teachers by demonstrating their professional ability to integrate all relevant information and make an informed decision to drive further instruction.

The development of teachers' ability to reflect on instruction is a significant topic in teacher education as this ability is considered to be an evidence of professional growth as reflective practitioners. Video analysis can be used as an educational tool to support candidates' instructional practice and to improve their pedagogical skills as they notice concrete pieces of evidence observed in the video. Referring to their instructional strategies and changes in student learning, candidates can demonstrate effectiveness of their teaching.

Brunvand (2010) suggests that candidates should practice noticing or identifying relevant aspects of classroom interaction as expert teachers would do. Candidates should be able to make connections between classroom interactions and a broader instructional context that the classroom events take place.

Also, candidates must use their knowledge to make informed decisions in instructional settings different from their own. Teacher candidates, however, may lack the knowledge of subject content and pedagogical methods to perform expert-like evaluation of their practice. In other words, candidates need to know what to look for and how to evaluate what has occurred in the video. This action of noticing and evaluation requires two types of cognition: selective attention and knowledge-based reasoning (Sherin, 2007).

"Selective attention" means one knows what is worth attending to and what is not. As so many things occur simultaneously in a classroom, one must choose where to look and what is worth paying close attention to. Selective attention is a strategic solution to avoid superficial or unproductive observation of classroom events. Research highlights that candidates' engagement in video analysis is increased when clear and concrete actions are prompted during video analysis.

"Knowledge-based reasoning" concerns the ways one justifies what has been noticed with one's knowledge and understanding of content and pedagogy. Referring to their content or pedagogical knowledge, candidates can realize that teacher knowledge and instructional practices are distinct but highly interrelated entities. Justifying their instructional strategies to enhance student learning is an educative practice in which candidates demonstrate their professional abilities with evidence of references to their knowledge as well as to their instructional practice.

Consider the commentary of Lauren, a beginning teacher, on her recorded lesson of literacy instruction with a third-grade struggling reader. Out of many things that took place in the video, she studied the student's behavior and noticed changes in her student's performance.

> With video observation, it was apparent that Megan needed help sounding out some of the compound words. She was able to identify the letter once the sound was made. She specifically recalled the "sh" and "th" sounds successfully from a previous lesson. This increased Megan's confidence and motivation. During this activity, I noticed that Megan seemed less frustrated with spelling. This is the most confident that I saw her when it came to spelling. I would like to continue motivating Megan to take her time while spelling. Megan should continue to practice sounds and spelling in order to increase her knowledge.

Based on her observation of the student's performance, she decided to modify her future instruction, and justified those changes using her knowledge of instructional strategies and student needs. In this specific case, those instructional changes would not have occurred if she reflected on her teaching only from her memory. By evaluating evidence from a series of observations in the video clips of her lesson, Lauren was able to modify her instruction to better meet her student's specific literacy needs.

Video conveys the complexity and subtlety of classroom teaching as it occurs in real time. However, video can be overwhelming if a viewer is new to teaching as well as to video analysis. Research recommends that video analysis be introduced earlier in teacher training and become a routinized task embedded in various courses of the teacher preparation programs. The complex task of video observation must be supported by explicit instruction, scaffolding, and guidance by experts. If paired with analysis of lesson plans, instructional materials, and student work samples, video analysis serves as a more concrete evidence of change or growth in candidates' clinical practice.

SUMMARY

In this chapter, we have reviewed current research on the use of video in teacher education and provided a strategic framework for effective video analysis. A helpful questionnaire was presented to aid teacher candidates in determining their level of background knowledge and understanding of video analysis as a teaching and learning tool.

We have also discussed methods of video analysis in teacher education, underscoring the need for experienced guidance, while noting some of the limitations in the process and implementation of video-based analysis in teacher education. Addressing the increasing role of video in teacher assessments, such as edTPA, the need for planning and guidance was emphasized and coupled with suggestions for teacher educators and candidates.

REFERENCES

Arya, P., Christ, T., & Chiu, M. M. (2014). Facilitation and teacher behavior: An analysis of literacy teachers' video-case discussions. *Journal of Teacher Education*, *65*(2), 111–127.

Baecher, L., & Kung, S. (2011). Jumpstart novice teachers' ability to analyze classroom video: Affordances of an online workshop. *Journal of Digital Learning in Teacher Education*, *28*(1), 16–26.

Baecher, L. H., & Tuten, J. (2011). Directed peer response in differentiated approaches to the video analysis of teaching. *Excelsior: Leadership in Teaching and Learning*, *5*(2), 30–43.

Berliner, D. C. (1986). In pursuit of the expert pedagogue. *Educational Researcher*, *15*, 5–13. doi:10.3102/0013189X015007007.

Blomberg, G., Sherin, M. G., Renkl, A., Glogger, I., & Seidel, T. (2014). Understanding video as a tool for teacher education: Investigating instructional strategies integrating video to promote reflection. *Instructional Science*, *42*(3), 443–463. doi:10.1007/s11251-013-9281-6.

Brunvand, S. (2010). Best practices for producing video content for teacher education. *Contemporary Issues in Technology and Teacher Education*, *10*(2), 247–256.

Coffey, A. M. (2014). Using video to develop skills in reflection in teacher education students. *Australian Journal of Teacher Education*, *39*(9), 86–97.

Fadde, P., & Sullivan, P. (2013). Using interactive video to develop preservice teachers' classroom awareness. *Contemporary Issues in Technology and Teacher Education*, *13*(2), 156–174.

Gaudin, G., & Charliès, S. (2015). Video viewing in teacher education and professional development: A literature review. *Educational Research Review*, *16*, 41–67.

Harford, J., MacRuairc, G., & McCartan, D. (2010). "Lights, camera, reflection": Using peer video to promote reflective dialogue among student teachers. *Teacher Development*, *14*(1), 57–68.

Koc, Y., Peker, D., & Osmanoglu, A. (2009). Supporting teacher professional development through online video case study discussions: An assemblage of preservice and inservice teachers and the case teacher. *Teaching and Teacher Education*, *25*(8), 1158–1168.

Maclean, R., & White, S. (2007). Video reflection and the formation of teacher identity in a team of pre-service and experienced teachers. *Reflective Practice: International and Multidisciplinary Perspectives*, *8*(1), 47–60. doi:10.1080/14623940601138949.

Marsh, B., Mitchell, N., & Adamczyk, P. (2009). Interactive video technology: Enhancing professional learning in initial teacher education. *Computers and Education*, *54*(3), 742–748.

McCullagh, J. F., Bell, I., & Corscadden, F. (2013). How does video analysis support student teachers in the very early stages of their initial teacher education? *Teacher Education Advancement Network Journal*, *5*(3), 39–51.

Newhouse, C. P., Lane, J., & Brown, C. (2007). Reflecting on teaching practices using digital video representation in teacher education. *Australian Journal of Teacher Education*, *32*(3), 51–62.

Rosaen, C. L., Lundeberg, M., Cooper, M., Fritzen, A., & Terpstra, M. (2008). Noticing noticing: How does investigation of video records change how teachers reflect on their experiences? *Journal of Teacher Education*, *59*(4), 347–360.

Rosaen, C. L., Lundeberg, M., Cooper, M., Fritzen, A., & Terpstra, M. (2010). Interns' use of video cases to problematize their practice: Crash, burn, and (maybe) learn. *Journal of Technology and Teacher Education*, *18*(3), 459–488.

Santagata, R., & Angelici, G. (2010). Studying the impact of the lesson analysis framework on preservice teachers' abilities to reflect on videos of classroom teaching. *Journal of Teacher Education, 61*(4), 339–349.

Seidel, T., Blomberg, G., & Renkl, A. (2013). Instructional strategies for using video in teacher education. *Teaching and Teacher Education, 34,* 56–65.

Sherin, M. G. (2007). The development of teachers' professional vision in video clubs. In R. Goldman, R. Pea, B. Barron, & S. J. Derry (Eds.), *Video research in the learning sciences* (pp. 383–395). Mahwah, NJ: Lawrence Erlbaum.

Sherin, M. G., & van Es, E. A. (2009). Effects of video club participation on teachers' professional vision. *Journal of Teacher Education, 60*(1), 20–37.

Stanford Center for Assessment, Learning and Equity. (2017). About edTPA. Retrieved from https://scale.stanford.edu/teaching/edtpa.

Tripp, T. R., & Rich, P. J. (2012). The influence of video analysis on the process of teacher change. *Teaching and Teacher Education, 28,* 728–739.

van Es, E. (2010). A framework for facilitating productive discussions in video club. *Educational Technology, 50*(1), 8–12.

Welsch, R., & Devlin, P. (2007). Developing preservice teachers' reflection: Examining the use of video. *Action in Teacher Education, 28*(4), 53–61.

Wiens, P. D., Hessberg, K., LoCasale-Crouch, J., & DeCoster, J. (2013). Using a standardized video-based assessment in a university teacher education program to examine preservice teachers knowledge related to effective teaching. *Teaching and Teacher Education, 33*(1), 24–33.

Video Recording and Analysis for edTPA

STEPHEN J. HERNANDEZ

ASSESSMENT OF PERFORMANCE-BASED TEACHING PRACTICE

The key to successfully passing edTPA (Educator Teacher Preparation Assessment) is the submission of video evidence of one's teaching. This chapter first discusses the evolving use of video in the assessment and analysis of preservice teachers. The chapter continues by providing you with insights into the use of video as a central component of an edTPA portfolio, with specific attention paid to the tasks and rubrics within edTPA that requires video evidence.

In addition, detail is provided regarding the impact video evidence has on the scoring one receives in each of the relevant rubrics. The chapter concludes with a rubric-by-rubric review of two edTPA portfolios and the impact the submitted video clips had on the individual candidates' scores. The first case study analyzes a portfolio with average rubric scores, while the second case study is of a high-scoring portfolio.

The process of procuring a teaching credential typically involves completing an approved teacher preparation program and passing several teacher certification exams including edTPA. Each state determines the evidence the prospective teacher must submit in order to be awarded the credential (Wilson, Hallam, Pecheone, & Moss, 2014). The states that require candidates to receive a passing score on an edTPA portfolio includes New York, Georgia, Hawaii, and Washington, with additional states planning the use of edTPA over the coming years.

While completing a teacher preparation program is a given across each state, the other measures of teaching competency can vary. These measures take on the form of skills-based assessments intended to measure content or pedagogical knowledge, some form of student teaching, and/or an actual assessment of teaching practice.

When it comes to skills-based assessments and other forms of psychometrics, researchers have detailed the many studies that documented the inconclusiveness of these types of assessments to anticipate teaching effectiveness. In general, there is insufficient validity regarding the impact of teacher certification on student achievement (Wilson et al., 2014).

As such, the move toward the use of evidence of teaching practice has been growing in support for a number of years now. In 2001, the National Research Council asked for qualifiers that included formal testing as well as "assessments of teaching performance in the classroom, of candidate's ability to work effectively with diverse learning needs and cultural backgrounds and in a variety of setting and of competencies that more directly relate to student learning" (National Research Council, 2001, p. 172).

This effort and the "call for assessment of knowledge in teaching practice" (Wilson et al., 2014, p. 3) has been reinforced in various reports, including one in 2005 by the National Academy of Education (Darling Hammond & Baratz-Showden, 2005). This was reinforced in 2008 by the National Research Council and its "call for indicators that go beyond testing" to include "assessment of teaching performance in the classroom" (Wilson et al., 2014, p. 3).

The use of video evidence, specifically recordings of student teaching in the classroom, has become central to the preservice teacher assessment process, particularly with the implementation of edTPA as a high-stakes measure of competency for those who seek teacher certification in a number of states. The question then becomes, what are the essential characteristics of a quality edTPA video? That question is answered in the following section.

EVIDENCE OF TEACHING PRACTICE IN EDTPA ASSESSMENT

As a preservice teacher (a candidate in edTPA parlance) you have several undertakings to accomplish on the way to becoming a successful educator. Initially, you need to develop and apply knowledge of subject matter, content standards, and subject-specific pedagogy. Next, you need to develop and apply knowledge of students, including their varied strengths, needs, and interests while also considering research and theory about how students learn. Finally, you need to reflect on, justify, and analyze evidence of the effects of instruction on student learning (Stanford Center for Assessment, Learning and Equity, 2013).

Together, these undertakings are incorporated into the edTPA assessment process within the context of five dimensions of teaching (Stanford Center for Assessment, Learning and Equity, 2016). Candidates' evidence within these five dimensions is evaluated and scored throughout the edTPA rubrics. As such, video evidence is potentially critical in the assessment of all five dimensions across the planning, instruction, and assessment tasks of edTPA.

Planning, Instruction, and Assessment

The first dimension of your teaching that is evaluated is the planning of instruction and assessment. This is where you establish the instructional and social context for student learning, and it includes lesson plans, instructional materials, and students' assignments and/or assessments.

As part of this first dimension, you must demonstrate how your plans align with content standards as well as the specific goals and objectives delineated for students with diverse learning needs, including those with disabilities and English Language Learners as well as students who are gifted and talented.

Furthermore, in your portfolio planning, you must note how your lesson plans build on students' prior academic learning and life experiences as well as how the intended instruction is differentiated to address student needs. In addition to the documented artifacts that help support your claims as detailed in the Context for Learning, lesson plans, instructional materials, and commentaries, you are able to illustrate the comprehensiveness of your planning through the video evidence of your instruction.

Instructing and Engaging Students in Learning

The second dimension being assessed in your edTPA portfolio is the instruction and engagement of students. This is where video evidence is front and center. In this dimension, you need to include in your portfolio one or two unedited video clips of 15–20 minutes from the learning segment.

The number of video clips and the permissible length vary, depending on the subject-specific handbook you are using in constructing your edTPA portfolio. In addition, this second dimension requires commentary analysis detailing how you have engaged the students in learning activities as well as a detailed commentary regarding subject-specific pedagogical strategies used by you to facilitate student learning.

Assessing Student Learning

Assessment of student learning is the third dimension that is evaluated in the context of your edTPA portfolio. You are evaluated on how well you have provided evidence of student learning. The evaluation of this third dimension rests on several measures. This includes

1. criteria you, as the edTPA candidate, have determined that would be an accurate representation of student learning;
2. the actual analysis of that learning by your students; and
3. an analysis of your teaching and the overall student learning process.

How you provide evidence of assessment and the evaluation of student learning varies from one subject-specific handbook to another, but in general, one has the option of including video, audio, or written feedback as evidence of student learning. In addition, you must discuss how you elicited and monitored student responses so as to develop within the students a deep understanding of the subject matter. This is the "feedback" component of the portfolio.

Analysis of Teaching Effectiveness

The fourth dimension being assessed through one's edTPA portfolio is an analysis of teaching effectiveness. The evidence of this dimension is addressed within the framework of commentaries for the planning, instruction, and assessment tasks. More specifically, in Task 1 (planning), you must justify your plans inclusive of your knowledge of your students' learning strengths and needs, as well as your understanding and application of relevant principles of research and theory.

In Task 2 (instruction), your analysis must explain and justify what aspects of the learning segment were effective, what were not, and what you would change. In Task 3, your analysis must use the assessment results to determine the next steps of instruction for your students with varied learning needs. As is the case with the first dimension, video illustrations of effective instruction are a key ingredient in how well one's portfolio is evaluated.

Academic Language Development

The fifth dimension of teaching in which you are evaluated is your ability to develop the use of academic language in students. For this dimension, you are evaluated based on your ability to support students' oral and written use of academic language to deepen subject matter understandings.

Your competency for this aspect of the portfolio is determined from the commentaries and videos that explain and provide evidence of how students demonstrated their use of academic language. This is done via examples in the student work samples and/or video recordings of your engagement with the students.

limensions of teaching are assessed through one's edTPA
r   g several sources of evidence that include various artifacts
and commentaries. Specifically, the planning task looks at the instructional and social context, lesson plans, instructional materials, student assignments, and the planning commentary. The instruction task relies on video clips of your teaching as well as what you write in your instructional commentary, while the assessment task looks at several aspects of your plan for assessment and the outcomes of your teaching.

The specific components that are evaluated from Task 3 of your portfolio include the evaluation criteria you decide would be used to analyze student learning and an actual analysis of student learning as well an analysis of the whole class assessment. In addition, samples of feedback to three students (two students in early childhood and one student in special education) are required along with a comprehensive assessment commentary.

As previously noted, the scores you will receive on your edTPA portfolio are reliant on a number of items. How well you score on these items will determine whether you receive a passing or failing score on your portfolio. Scores are assigned to your work within the realm of 13–18 rubrics, depending on the subject-specific handbook that is being used. According to edTPA, the scores you receive are indicative of your readiness to teach and are described as follows:

1. A level one score is representative of the knowledge and skills of a seriously struggling candidate who is not ready to teach.
2. A level two score represents the knowledge and skills of a candidate who is possibly ready to teach.
3. A level three score represents the knowledge and skills of a candidate who is qualified to teach.
4. A level four score represents a candidate with a solid foundation of knowledge and skills for a beginning teacher.
5. A level five score represents the advanced skills and abilities of a candidate very well qualified and ready to teach.

As described earlier, the progression from a score of one to five is indicative of the candidate's expanding repertoire of skills and strategies, as well as a deepening of their rationale for what was taught, and a reflection on how effective the teaching was. In general, a score of one is illustrative of a candidate who lacks an individualized, student-specific focus, and engages in fragmented and indiscriminate instruction, rather than teaching that is integrated, intentional, and well executed.

With this in mind, it is not overstating the fact to say that the most critical evidence of your edTPA portfolio is the video(s) submitted for Task 2 and possibly Task 3. For, no matter how much work is put into the planning of the lessons in Task 1, if you do not execute those plans well and there is a lack of video evidence of effective teaching, the integrity of the portfolio will suffer, potentially beyond repair.

Let's now review those practices and strategies that are necessary for creating effective video footage for an edTPA portfolio.

STRATEGIES FOR EFFECTIVE VIDEO RECORDING

What are the features of a quality edTPA video? For one, you do not need to produce an award-winning movie! This is not a cinematography contest. It is necessary though for you to create a video that is of sufficient clarity in sight and sound so the scorer can easily discern what occurred in your classroom. The scorer needs to see you engaged with the students in a manner that is consistent with the requirements for the five rubrics in Task 2 (instruction) as well as for the rubrics in Task 3 (assessment) that allow for video evidence to be cited.

Before we review each of the rubrics in Task 2, remember a couple of particulars regarding the edTPA videotaping process. First, practice using the video equipment at home before you actually begin recording any lessons.

Next, make sure you have consent forms from students and adults who may appear in the video. Once you have the consent forms in hand and know who can and cannot appear in the video, set up the camera in a "video-friendly" location in the classroom or another appropriate instructional setting and engage in some practice taping before you actually record your lessons.

Establishing a video-friendly setting in the classroom means organizing the room for filming. Position the camera in the room so the footage will provide the scorer with the visual evidence of you and the focus students engaged in the teaching and learning process. If possible, move the teacher's desk to a location off-camera and make sure students and adults who have not provided consent are placed out of camera range in the classroom.

Setting up the video equipment before recording and then engaging in practice videotaping will allow you and your students to become comfortable with the presence of the equipment and give you the opportunity to refine your presence while on camera. Once you begin to videotape your edTPA lessons, try to record the entire set of three to five lessons. Doing so will give you a good deal of recorded material to choose from.

The additional footage will also provide you with "backup" in the event there is a technical or quality-related problem with the video. The additional material may also be necessary in the event there is the need for a retake of all or a portion of the portfolio.

This last suggestion might be the most important practical step you take in creating your portfolio—make sure to save, in multiple locations (flash drives, hard drive, etc.), each and every file, including the video clip(s) you create for your edTPA submission. The last thing you want to have happen is to find out that your videotaped evidence has been corrupted, damaged, or lost. Frequently saving your files, in more than one location, is an absolute necessity.

Remember that the submitted video clip(s) must show you engaging the students during the lessons. At minimum, a visual image of your face must appear in at least one video clip in order to confirm your identity. Even better, make sure that the video(s) illustrate you and your students engaged in active instruction and learning. More information regarding this is noted in the following text.

It is very important to remember to make sure there is no public sharing or posting on public venues of the video, and do not share the video content with people who are not involved with the edTPA assessment process. The video clips must be unedited and must be of the appropriate length, as specified in the applicable subject-specific handbook. Finally, the video clip(s) must feature you teaching your subject area.

More specifically, as you engage your students in instruction, you need to ask yourself a number of questions when deciding what segment of your video footage you will submit as the evidence:

1. How did you demonstrate respect, rapport, and responsiveness to students with varied needs and backgrounds while also challenging students to engage in learning?
2. How did you elicit and build on student responses in ways that developed and deepened their content understanding?
3. In what ways did you connect new content to your students' prior academic learning and personal, cultural, or community assets during the instructional process?
4. Did you refer to examples from the video clips in the responses to the prompts? Particularly,

   - Did you explain how your instruction engaged students?
   - Did you describe how your instruction linked students' prior academic learning and personal, cultural, and community assets with new learning?

5. Finally, what kinds of learning tasks actively engaged the students in the central focus of the learning segment?

Once you have identified where the evidence exists in your video footage, you then need to crop the clip(s) for the portfolio. Remember, the submitted video clip(s) cannot be edited. This means the video evidence must consist of continuous recording of your teaching.

portant for you to recognize that the 15- to 20-minute video
im____   /evidence of your teaching and learning as required across
the five rubrics of Task 2 (instruction) along with possibly an additional
three rubrics for Task 3 (assessment). For that reason, you must select
video clip(s) that illustrate multiple approaches of you engaging students
in the learning process, as described in the Task 1 planning commentary.

While you may question the ability to include everything you need
to demonstrate in just 15–20 minutes or so of video footage, you must
address the rubric requirements as specified by edTPA through well-
planned and skillfully executed lessons. Table 2.1 presents a tool you
can use as an aide in planning the use of your videotaped evidence.

You should refer to the chart in table 2.1 as you watch your videos to
determine where you see evidence of the required elements in each of
the prompts in Task 2 and possibly in Task 3. Determining in advance
the location of the video evidence prior to writing the commentaries

Table 2.1 Checklist of video clips to address relevant rubrics

Task	Rubric	Lesson 1	Lesson 2	Lesson 3
Task 2 (instruction) identifying appropriate video	Rubric 6: learning environment			
	Rubric 7: engaging students in learning			
	Rubric 8: deepening student learning			
	Rubric 9: subject-specific pedagogy			
	Rubric 10: analyzing teaching effectiveness			
Task 3 (assessment)	Rubric 11: analysis of student learning			
	Rubric 12: providing feedback to guide learning			
	Rubric 14: analyzing students' language use and content understanding			

Source: Stephen Hernandez.

lessens the time spent figuring out where your video evidence is. Doing so will make the writing of your commentaries less time-consuming.

You do not submit this chart with your portfolio. It is simply an aide for determining where in the candidates' video the evidence exists for each of the rubrics noted in the chart.

Using the data noted in the chart, you will then time-stamp where in the provided video clip(s) the evidence exists that you are citing in the portfolio commentary. You want to lead the scorer to where the illustrations are that support your claims in the commentaries.

Failing to accurately time-stamp is like providing driving directions to someone without telling where and when to make a left- or right-hand turn. The more specific the directions are, the less likely the driver will get lost. The same holds true for your commentary and the directions you are providing the scorer when he or she is viewing your video clip(s).

Now that you have a good sense as to the importance of the video evidence in the construction of your edTPA portfolio, let's now take a look at two portfolios and see the impact their video evidence had on their edTPA scores in rubrics 6–10 in Task 2 as well as in rubrics 11, 12, and 14 in Task 3.

A CASE STUDY OF EFFECTIVE VIDEO ANALYSIS: TOM

This section and the next one provide you with an analysis of two scored edTPA portfolios. The analysis focuses on the rubrics in Tasks 2 and 3 where video was submitted as evidence. The first portfolio, submitted by Tom, received a total score of 43 out of 75 and is consistent with the national average of 44.2 for 15 rubric portfolios (Stanford Center for Assessment, Learning and Equity, 2016). The second portfolio, submitted by Jessica, received a total score of 64.

Getting back to Tom and his portfolio, he received scores of 3 in nine rubrics, scores of 4 in two rubrics, and scores of 2 in four rubrics. Specifically, Tom's scores in the rubrics that used video evidence are as follows: In Task 2, he scored a 3 for rubrics 6, 7, and 8, along with a 4 in rubric 9. He scored a 2 for rubric 10. In Task 3, Tom received scores of 3 in rubrics 11 and 12 and a score of 2 in rubric 14.

Remember, candidates need to receive a minimum score of 3 in order for their work to be considered indicative of someone who is qualified to teach. A score of 2 on the other hand represents the knowledge and skills of a candidate who is possibly ready to teach. Unless you receive a couple of rubric scores above a 3, scores of 2 in more than just 4–5 rubrics will likely result in a failing portfolio.

In Task 2, rubric 6 (learning environment) pertains to the candidate's ability to demonstrate a positive learning environment that supports students' engagement in learning. In this rubric Tom received a perfectly acceptable score of 3.

As noted in the subject-specific *Understanding Rubric Level Progressions* guidebook (Stanford Center for Assessment, Learning and Equity, 2016), a candidate receives this score as a result of video evidence illustrating the engagement of students in a respectful manner where they establish a rapport with the learners. That respect and rapport created by Tom allowed the students to easily communicate with him. His score is also indicative of Tom being able to facilitate a positive learning environment.

Why didn't Tom receive a higher score in this rubric? A review of the difference between a score of 3 and 4 on rubric 6 rests on the candidate challenging the students to engage in higher-order thinking or the application of new learning.

Demonstrating just respect, rapport, and the creation of a positive learning environment, while not illustrating the challenging of student learning, will result in a maximum score of 3 on this rubric.

Rubric 7 (engaging students in learning) addresses how you as the candidate engage students in the learning process. Tom received another 3 for this rubric, primarily as a result of the video evidence illustrating him using strategies designed to engage the students in content-appropriate learning, which is related to the students' prior knowledge and experiences.

Rubric 8 (deepening student learning) addresses the candidate's ability to deepen student learning. On this rubric, Tom again scored a 3. This score was achieved primarily through Tom illustrating the structuring of the learning process in a way that prompted the students to apply new knowledge and skills in concert with the established goals of the lessons.

In addition, the video recording showed Tom providing accurate and specific feedback to his students. A score of 4 would have resulted if, in addition to the evidence noted earlier, he had been able to prompt the students to apply the knowledge learned in the portfolio lessons.

Rubric 9 (subject-specific pedagogy) addresses subject-specific pedagogy, and in this area Tom scored the best out of all of the other Task 2 rubrics, receiving a 4 out of 5. He was able to achieve this score by showing in his video the use of instructional strategies that foster the students' progress toward achieving the learning segment goals.

Even more specifically, his score reflected his ability to promote a deeper understanding of the content in his students through guided practice and self-directed learning.

Tom's score on rubric 10 (analysis of teaching effectiveness) was only 2. As noted earlier, a score below 3 represents the skills of someone who is possibly ready to teach. In Tom's case, his portfolio was superficial in its ability to propose changes in future learning experiences. In addition, the changes he did propose were not directly related to the students and their knowledge, as illustrated in the video.

In addition to the required use of video evidence for Task 2 (instruction), candidates can use video evidence in their analysis of the portfolio's assessment results (Task 3). Specifically, candidates in some content areas are able to illustrate their ability to analyze student learning (rubric 11—analysis of student learning) and provide feedback to a student to guide their learning (rubric 12—providing feedback to guide further learning) as well as convey their analysis of the students' use of language (rubric 14).

Tom did use video evidence for all three of these rubrics, with sufficient success in rubrics 11 and 12. He was not so proficient in documenting student language use for rubric 14. For all three of these rubrics, Tom included an additional video clip as an artifact for Task 3.

For rubric 11, Tom's score of 3 demonstrated an analysis that draws on his knowledge of students' performance along with the students' strengths and needs. Tom also scored a 3 on rubric 12, with his video clip illustrating detailed feedback to the students. When it came to Tom's ability to analyze the student's language use, the rubric 14 (analyzing language use) score of 2 is indicative of limited relationship of the identified language use to the learning segment's learning goals.

In conclusion, Tom's use of video, and his commentary analysis, provided him with just enough evidence to receive a level three score in five of the video-applicable rubrics. His score of 4 in rubric 9 just barely offset the two rubrics (#10 and #14) with scores of 2.

On review, Tom's scores in the Task 3 rubrics may have been improved with better analysis of his available evidence. Instead of using a different video clip for his Task 3 evidence, he may have had more illustrative video from his Task 2 video clip, or he could have chosen to not use video evidence at all for Task 3.

The next case study is a contrast to Tom's and provides an example as to how just 20 minutes of video can result in a high score on all eight video-relevant rubrics.

A CASE STUDY OF EFFECTIVE VIDEO ANALYSIS: JESSICA

This analysis is a portfolio that received a much higher score than Tom. In this case, Jessica received a total edTPA score of 64 (out of a maximum of 75). Her portfolio use of video evidence received scores of 4.0 (out of 5) on rubrics 6, 7, 9, and 10, a score of 5 on rubric 8 in Task 2 (instruction), and scores of 4, 5, and 4, respectively, on rubrics 11, 12, and 14 in Task 3.

As already noted, rubric 6 pertains to the candidate's ability to demonstrate a positive learning environment that supports students' engagement in learning. As stated earlier, Jessica received a score of 4 for this rubric.

This score is indicative of the candidate creating an instructional environment that facilitated a positive learning environment that provides both support and challenge for the students as it pertains to the lesson objectives for the learning goal. In addition, the video footage illustrated the encouragement of and existence of mutual respect and rapport among students and between the students and the candidate.

Jessica's ability to engage her students in the learning process resulted in her receiving a score of 4 on rubric 7. This score resulted from the fact that Jessica was able to demonstrate her engagement with the students in a way that facilitated their learning and made connections between the students' prior learning and their personal, cultural, and community assets.

In addition, Jessica was able to clearly demonstrate the use of appropriate scaffolding that integrated the objectives of the learning goal with one another and provided evidence of smooth transitions from one learning activity to another.

Deepening student learning is the focus of rubric 8, and on this rubric Jessica scored a 5 out of 5. The candidate's score resulted from the inclusion of evidence in the clips showing students being provided with the opportunity to engage in self-monitoring and self-correction. In addition, Jessica provided the students with the opportunity to build on the knowledge and skills related to the desired learning outcomes.

For rubric 9 candidates need to provide evidence of how they support learning as it relates to the subject content. Jessica scored a 4 in this rubric by explicitly demonstrating her ability to provide the students with appropriate instructional strategies, supports, and materials that then capitalize on student learning.

Finally, rubric 10, the last one in Task 2, requires candidates to analyze their own teaching effectiveness and asks how the candidates used evidence to evaluate and change their own teaching practice to then meet students' varied learning needs.

As with the majority of the rubrics in Task 2 (instruction), Jessica received a score of 4 on this rubric. She accomplished this by proposing changes to her teaching that relate directly to the strengths and needs of the student, as illustrated in the video footage submitted.

As noted in Tom's case, candidates can also use video evidence when it comes to their work for Task 3. Jessica did just that, providing video evidence from her Task 2 in analyzing student learning and guiding student learning from feedback in Task 3. Jessica received scores of 4, 5, and 4, respectively, for rubrics 11, 12, and 14. Remember, Jessica was able to effectively illustrate her skills across eight rubrics in less than 20 minutes of video footage!

On rubric 11, Jessica was able to use details regarding her students' strengths and needs as well as the levels and types of supports they need. Specifically, she conveyed specific knowledge of her students as it relates to their progress toward achieving the learning goal.

That level of detail paid off handsomely with regard to rubric 12 where she scored a 5. An analysis of the score and her portfolio shows that Jessica was able to explicitly provide feedback to the students and specifically relates the feedback to the students' prior learning.

Finally, Jessica employed video evidence from her Task 2 video in her analysis for rubric 14, the only other rubric in Task 3 that can cite video evidence. For this rubric, Jessica scored a 4 out of 5 as a result of identifying and describing the video evidence illustrating the student's use of the relevant language functions, applicable vocabulary, and the associated language demand of discourse.

Key here is the evidence showing not just the use of language functions and vocabulary but also the appropriate use of discourse (or syntax) as an associated language demand. In addition, Jessica's score in rubric 14 was a result of her analysis, including specific information noting the growth and/or struggles of students in the development of content understandings.

To summarize, Jessica was deliberate and focused on creating a high-content video. Her video provided evidence of her clearly establishing respect and rapport, promoting an appropriate and effective learning environment, and engaging students in a manner that facilitated high-quality and in-depth learning in a supportive environment.

In addition, the video exhibited her analysis of the students' performance while also reflecting on her teaching, student-directed feedback, and their use of content-relevant language. Accomplishing this took advance preparation, planning, and a continual focus on maximizing the use of video evidence to address the required components of her portfolio. In the end, Jessica's work paid off.

SUMMARY

The primary purpose of this chapter is to provide the reader with a detailed guide on the use of video footage in the creation of a high-quality edTPA portfolio. Note must be taken that no one component of one's portfolio is independent of the other. A poorly designed set of lesson plans will be reflected in the video footage taken of those lessons.

And while it has been previously stated that a well-developed planning task, if not reflected in the video evidence, can result in a low score, the fact remains that candidates need to pursue the goal of producing a high-quality portfolio overall and avoid the trap of attempting to skirt around the work in any one of the tasks or rubric requirements.

The guidance provided in this chapter has provided effective support to teacher candidates preparing edTPA portfolios. Note though that the guidance, suggestions, and strategies discussed here will not result in a high score if the candidate is not committed to producing a well-developed portfolio. Use the information provided here as an aide in the process, not as a substitute for your own pedagogical insight and knowledge.

REFERENCES

Darling Hammond, L., & Baratz-Showden, J. (2005). *A good teacher in every classroom: Preparing the highly qualified teachers our children deserve.* San Francisco, CA: John Wiley & Sons.

National Research Council. (2001). *Testing teacher candidates: The role licensure tests in improving teacher quality.* Washington, DC: The National Academies Press.

Stanford Center for Assessment, Learning and Equity. (2013). *edTPA Field Test: Summary report.* Palo Alto, CA.

Stanford Center for Assessment, Learning and Equity. (2016). *Educative assessment & meaningful support. 2015 edTPA administrative report.* Palo Alto, CA.

Wilson, M., Hallam, P. J., Pecheone, R. L., & Moss, P. A. (2014). Evaluating the validity of portfolio assessments for licensure decisions. *Education Policy Analysis Archives, 22*(6). Retrieved October 14, 2016, from http://dx.doi.org/10.14507/epaa.v22n6.2014.

Collaborative Strategies for edTPA Video Recording and Analysis

Nikki L. Josephs, Arleen Schefflein, and Robert Cooper

The Educator Teacher Preparation Assessment (edTPA) has been adopted as the final assessment for teacher licensure by many states. Although there is a subject-specific handbook for each teacher licensure certification, all edTPA submissions require teacher candidates to complete a self-analysis of their teaching with the use of a video recording. It is during this video recording task that teacher candidates demonstrate their ability to instruct classroom students and provide evidence of student engagement.

This chapter focuses on the use of video analysis and collaborative strategies during the edTPA preparation. The intended audience of this chapter includes preservice teacher candidates (TCs), cooperating classroom teachers (CTs), and college/university field supervisors (FSs) or mentors who work with preservice TCs during fieldwork experiences.

To promote the effective use of video analysis in the process of preparing and submitting edTPA portfolios, this chapter focuses on the materials needed for the video component of the edTPA. This includes a review of the task directions, scoring rubrics, and equipment requirements.

Additional information is discussed regarding the roles of the cooperating classroom teacher, college/university FS or mentor, and peers in the preparation of the video analysis portion of the edTPA submission. Specifically, information is given on how each member of the team can provide support to the TC in the form of practice video analysis methods before the official edTPA submission process has begun.

Video analysis has been shown to be effective in the improvement of the ability of preservice teachers to pay attention to and use knowledge-based reasoning for instructional decisions (Kleinknecht & Groschner, 2016; Rich & Hannafin, 2008; Star & Strickland, 2008). It has also been shown to provide more reflective descriptions of teacher and student actions during instruction (Santagata & Guarino, 2011).

As such, the video component is an integral portion of the edTPA. Candidates are required to video record aspects of their submitted learning segments that highlight student activities related to the task requirements. Each candidate should thoroughly review the correlated edTPA handbook and the *Making Good Choices: A Support Guide for edTPA Candidates* (Stanford Center for Assessment, Learning, and Equity, 2016) for complete directions, scoring rubrics, and frequently asked questions.

Readers will also find embedded *Instructional Spotlights* (figures 3.1–3.4), where aspects of the video recording and analysis portion are highlighted with examples using the role of the FS, cooperating teacher, and peers in the process. In addition, each *Spotlight* includes author-created materials to assist the target audience through different collaborative activities in the video preparation process.

ROLE OF THE FIELD SUPERVISOR

In most teacher certification programs, an FS is assigned to work with a TC. The FS is responsible for supporting the candidate by offering feedback from classroom observations, teaching the key pedagogical components during seminar sessions, providing specific strategies for effective classroom management, and modeling the myriad teacher dispositions necessary for classroom success.

The FS plays an essential role in overall preservice teacher preparation and is particularly important during the edTPA video-recording process. Though the program structures and responsibilities differ across teacher preparation programs, the FS is typically an individual responsible for observing and working with the candidate throughout the field/practicum experience.

One of the most important aspects of effective teacher observation is that it is student focused. FSs can provide feedback to the candidate with a focus on the things he or she does well and how to improve instruction to ensure that classroom students succeed academically, emotionally, and socially. Also, the FS can foster the growth of a candidate in many ways and can be especially effective when using video as a tool to inspire reflection and spark pedagogical improvement.

During the initial weeks of the student/supervised teaching, practicum, or clinical practice time frame, the FS should provide the candidate with opportunities to practice the skill of viewing video clips to provide meaningful reflection.

Santagata and Angelici (2010) found that when candidates are provided focused questions and instruction on what to focus when viewing video of classroom instruction, they are much more likely to create more detailed and focused commentary. FSs may choose to use time early in the field/clinical experience to have candidates practice viewing and responding to guided questions as a means of preparing for their later edTPA submission.

It is recommended that FSs encourage candidates to begin to video record their classroom interactions early in the field/clinical experience or practicum for several reasons:

1. Self-reflection from video recording is one of the clearest ways for a candidate to assess his or her performance in front of children (Star & Strickland, 2008).

2. The candidate may discern the best ways to demonstrate pedagogy, highlight student responses, and view the classroom.
3. When the candidate begins to video record in the classroom early in the experience, the students may get used to having a video camera in operation during instruction.

With these preliminary steps completed, any subsequent lessons may be conducted naturally and any undue stress on the part of students and the candidate may be lessened, when the time comes to formally video record for edTPA submission.

In addition to providing support for video recording early in the experience, the FS should use edTPA prompts to spark discussion of the practice videos to provide the candidate with opportunities to speak and write in the language of edTPA. It is a fair and legal approach to edTPA preparation for the FS and candidates to be familiar with and practice the use of edTPA terms as a means of professional reflection.

If the FS has a seminar course with a few TCs, it may be beneficial to provide the group with example videos, either of the candidates or of other published teaching segments, so the candidates can engage in the shared viewing of these videos and use edTPA prompts and scoring rubrics to practice speaking and writing in the language of edTPA.

As part of a seminar class session or advance preparation assignment, the FS may choose to use a video segment to illustrate specific examples of teacher behavior and student interaction in the classroom. This type of exercise can provide the candidate opportunities to practice the use of the language of edTPA when responding to the prompts on the assessment.

When developing this type of activity, it is suggested that the FS uses his or her own discretion regarding the length, subject area(s), learning target, and amount of times to view the video clip. Candidates may be instructed to view the clip a specific number of times as they complete the prompts, if needed.

Instructional Spotlight 1: example activity to engage teacher candidate in use of edTPA language

Suggested prompts

- Describe how this teacher's instruction linked students' prior academic learning and personal, cultural, and community assets with new learning.
- Explain how this teacher elicited and built on student responses to promote thinking.
- Explain how you modeled the essential strategy and supported students as they practiced or applied the strategy.
- What changes would you make to this lesson to better support student learning?

FIGURE 3.1
Source: Nikki L. Josephs, Arleen Schefflein, Robert Cooper

ROLE OF THE COOPERATING TEACHER

Cooperating teachers (CTs) serve a crucial role in the preparation and development of preservice TCs. They model excellence in teacher pedagogy and the positive dispositions novice teachers need to be able to reach all students. Once again, one of the most important aspects of effective teacher observation is that it be student focused. CTs should emphasize the aspects candidates do well and how they can improve their instruction.

Feedback and genuine support from the in-classroom CT can help to forge a positive working relationship with the candidate and may serve as the anchor to a TC's success. CTs can also be an invaluable asset during the video-recording component of the edTPA required tasks.

The CT can serve as the operator of the camera and can provide opportunities for the candidate to practice video recording of instructional segments. Also, the CT can give the candidate video analysis checklists in which to analyze their practice video recordings in preparation for the final edTPA submission (see example checklist in the section Creation of a Checklist).

The CT and the candidate can use the field/clinical experience/practicum, to practice video recording to inform the conversations around classroom lesson planning and student learning. The CT can provide the candidate multiple opportunities to create challenging learning tasks that support the classroom Context for Learning, which is required for the edTPA Task 1 (planning).

After each practice lesson, the CT and the candidate can review the videos and discuss areas of strength and improvement, with a focus on how to best address the classroom students' needs. In addition, these practice videos can help to launch the nuanced changes and shifts to pedagogy that may further the growth and maturity of the candidate.

For example, during Week 3 of the field experience, practicum, or clinical practice, the CT may choose to help the candidate focus on demonstrating and assessing student engagement on a specific learning task. The CT may allow the candidate time to create a mini lesson plan and video record the classroom interactions. Together, they can use a video analysis tool, like the edTPA scoring rubrics (available at www.edtpa.com) or self-created behavior checklists, to analyze the execution of the candidate's and students' behavior during the practice lesson plan.

To help facilitate the follow-up reflective conversation, the CT may choose to use the prompts and/or rubrics found in the correlated edTPA handbook and/or *Making Good Choices* (Stanford Center for Assessment, Learning, and Equity, 2016) to reinforce best practices with which the candidate should be familiar. The purpose of this type of activity is to assist the ability of TCs to view the intricacy in the classroom events.

Candidates should work with their cooperating teacher to identify areas for improvement and practice video-based reflective writing. Note that no practice lesson where feedback has been given to the candidate can be the final submission for the edTPA.

Directions:

1. Watch the assigned video clip.
2. Reflect on the events and provide a written commentary on the skills demonstrated in the video.
3. Replay and review as needed.

Elements of Classroom Management	Time Stamp(s)	Detailed Comments
Use of praise		
Use of error correction		
Questioning technique(s)		
Teacher/student movement patterns		
Use of wait time		
Provide varied opportunities to respond		
Provide students with feedback		

FIGURE 3.2

Instructional Spotlight 2a: video-based reflective practice: what classroom management elements can you observe?

Source: Nikki L. Josephs, Arleen Schefflein, Robert Cooper

Directions:

1. Watch the assigned video clip.
2. Reflect on the Instructional Practices used throughout the lesson.
3. Replay and review as needed.

Instructional Practice	
• Gaining/maintaining student attention • Giving instructions • Establishing routines • Accessing prior knowledge • Using technology • Developing concept understanding • Checking understanding	

Element	Time Stamp(s)	Observation
Giving instructions	03:27	In small groups, students are all seated at table near the teacher when he or she gives specific instructions about follow-up to lesson activity.

FIGURE 3.3

Instructional Spotlight 2b: observing instructional practice

Source: Nikki L. Josephs, Arleen Schefflein, Robert Cooper

EFFECTIVE USE OF PEER SUPPORT

Peers can be valuable assets in the edTPA video-recording and analysis process. Peers can offer multiple opportunities to capture, view, and discuss video data that are obtained during classroom instruction. If given the opportunity to view the recordings of their peers, candidates may have the opportunity to offer critique, with focus on areas of strength and improvement, and the ability to refine each other's teaching practices in a collegial manner.

During these discourses, candidates should be encouraged to explain and justify instructional decisions and allow their peers to make certain that these decisions are correct and clearly presented.

The Practicum Seminar can provide candidates an opportunity to engage in reflective dialogue about their lesson plans and video recordings. As a peer coach, candidates can be trained by the FS or the cooperating teacher to use checklists or scoring rubrics to offer suggestions on ways to support and improve classroom practices based on their own experiences.

By offering this informal support and critique, candidates can provide additional assistance and explanations where the cooperating teacher and/or FS cannot. Together, candidates can aid in the successful completion of the edTPA.

Although it may be an uncomfortable experience initially, candidates may appreciate having the opportunity to watch themselves and their peers in action. Peer viewing of video-recorded classroom instruction can be a powerful tool in learning to become a reflective educator. Peer support can help candidates generate ideas of how to teach concepts in new and engaging ways. The use of peers and video recording can transform abstract theory into concrete conceptualizations.

Peer support can be an essential tool in the video-recording and analysis portion of the edTPA. During this assessment process, TCs can offer each other guidance, support, and critique that cannot be formally offered by the FS or cooperating teacher. One way peers can offer instructional support to each other is to view and critique each other's teaching from a practice video recording.

edTPA Task Analysis Worksheet		
Category	Criteria	Time-Stamp of Examples
Learning Environment	Interactions between teacher and students are respectful	
	Students communicate easily with the candidate	
	Students willing to share their responses	
	Students show attentive listening to one another	
	Students are asked to think deeply about their responses	
Engaging Students in Learning	Teacher makes connections between prior and current learning.	
	Students are engaged in tasks that require them to use the essential skills and strategies	
	Structures to support student learning are provided	
	Students are asked to draw on personal/cultural/community experiences	
Deepening Student Learning	Students elaborate responses to content ideas	
	Teacher and students build on the ideas of others	
Subject-Specific Pedagogy	Models the essential strategy or skill	
	Students have opportunity to practice with teacher guidance	

FIGURE 3.4

Instructional Spotlight 3: task analysis worksheet

Source: Nikki L. Josephs, Arleen Schefflein, Robert Cooper

Figure 3.4 highlights an example activity where peers can use a Task Analysis Worksheet to practice the use of providing evidence from the video using time stamps.

Prior to using a tool like this task analysis worksheet, each candidate should be familiar with the categories and edTPA criteria needed for their learning segment. Be sure to carefully review the appropriate edTPA handbook.

Next, candidates should video record themselves teaching a lesson. The lesson should include a distinct opening, middle, and closing activity, and preferably include opportunities for classroom student engagement. After this, the candidate should select (or be assigned) a peer viewer, someone who will view the recorded segment and mark any edTPA task criteria they see demonstrated in video by placing the corresponding time stamp in the aligning column.

Together, the candidates can review the completed worksheet and the peer viewer can offer areas of strength and improvement for future teaching opportunities.

ROLE OF THE TEACHER CANDIDATE

The TC should be the leader of his or her own edTPA submission. It should be the sole responsibility of the TC to decide which learning segments to create and subsequently submit for formal review. Along with support from the FS, cooperating teacher, and peers, the TC should be able to demonstrate his or her full understanding of the edTPA requirements and use the video-recorded segments of instruction to demonstrate student learning and engagement.

The following sections are an overview of how TCs can continue to make good decisions regarding the video-recording and analysis portion of edTPA submission.

Deciding What to Video Record

The edTPA requires the TC to create a unit plan of three to five lessons. Although the edTPA content and lesson plan format of these lessons may vary across teacher licensure areas, it is from these lessons that the TC should select at least two learning segments to use for the video-recording portion of the assessment.

As mentioned in a previous section, it is recommended that the TC and the cooperating teacher coordinate efforts to video record lessons to be submitted for edTPA. There are a few options available for TCs in terms of preparing the video analysis portion of the assessment:

1. The TC may choose to video record every occurrence of his or her teaching throughout the student/supervised teaching, practicum, or clinical practice.
2. The TC may opt to video record the entire learning segment.
3. The TC may video record only selected portions of the learning segment to be submitted for the edTPA.

The final decision of what to video record should be left to the TC. However, it is recommended to video most, if not all, of the unit lessons to be considered for edTPA submission. The main reason for this suggestion is that the TC will be able to choose the best segments from the several hours of teaching—essentially demonstrating examples of active student engagement, multiple pedagogical approaches, and effective student-centered activities.

The criteria for selection of the most effective video-recorded learning segments should be based on the recognition of the best practices, but more specifically on a solid working knowledge of the edTPA rubrics that govern the assigned tasks (i.e., rubrics 6–10). It is important that TCs have a thorough understanding of those scoring rubrics and commentary prompts during the advanced planning stages.

In addition to being familiar with the scoring rubrics and commentary prompts, TCs may choose to use a checklist to ensure they include all relevant components of the assigned edTPA tasks.

Creation of a Checklist

Creating a checklist for completion can be a valuable use of time for all TCs. A checklist can provide the TC with specific guidelines to

Table 3.1 Example of a checklist

Completed	Video analysis tasks
	Read through rubrics in the edTPA handbook
	Reviewed pages of "Making Good Choices"
	Checked edTPA handbook for exact file naming convention, formatting, number of files, and length requirements
	Identified a recording device to use (FLIP video, iPhone, camera, etc.) and found a clear spot in the classroom to set up device
	Obtained permission from the parents/guardians of the students and from the adults who will appear in the video
	Recorded myself teaching ALL the lessons in which I actively engage and interact with students within the learning segment (three to five consecutive lessons)
	Watched my video(s) multiple times and decided which one or two video clips to use, and made backup copies of the video(s)
	Video elements
	Did not include the name, city, state, or district of the school in my video
	Used only first names for all students who appear in the videos
	Made sure that the final clip(s) is/are continuous and unedited
	Made sure the video(s) is/are in the correct format: one or two files, no more than 20 minutes total running time (.flv, .asf, .qt, .mov, .mpg, .mpeg, .avi, .wmv, .mp4, .m4v)

Source: Nikki L. Josephs, Arleen Schefflein, Robert Cooper

organize and guide the efficiency of the edTPA tasks. Also, the checklist can serve as an accountability tool to ensure the TC has completed all required components of the video-recording and analysis task.

See table 3.1 for an example edTPA checklist. In addition to creating and using a checklist to guide the edTPA tasks, TCs may/should choose to pay close attention to the preparation of the classroom during video recording.

Preparing the Classroom for Video Recording

Per the edTPA handbook, there is no requirement or expectation to create a professional-quality video production. However, it is important that TCs provide video-recorded segments that have good sound and visual quality for official edTPA submission.

TCs should ensure that submitted video segments enable the reviewer to examine clear demonstrations of teacher and student behaviors during the instructional segment(s). It is recommended that TCs read the correlated edTPA handbook carefully to be sure to video record and submit clips that are the appropriate length and feature the teaching and learning goals emphasized for their subject area.

Preparing the classroom for the video recording is simple but must be well planned. As suggested by the edTPA *Making Good Choices* (Stanford Center for Assessment, Learning, and Equity, 2016), TCs should practice the optimal location for the video equipment to ensure good sound and visual quality.

TCs should think about where the locus of instruction will be and where the students will be during the learning segments. Be sure to place the camera in a location that allows for the TC and the students to be seen and heard clearly.

During the preparation of the classroom phase, the TC and cooperating teacher can ensure the aisles are clear for ease of movement throughout the classroom. It may take some practice to find the ideal camera position in the classroom.

The cooperating teacher and the TC may choose to use the practice video-recording sessions to discern the best location for the camera. See the previous segment on the role of the cooperating teacher (pp. 41–43) for details regarding video-recording practice sessions.

Students without Permission to Appear on Video

It is essential for TCs to obtain permission for video recording in the classroom. Please review the edTPA handbook for complete details and instructions for obtaining appropriate permissions to video record. However, there may be instances where permission cannot be obtained for all students in the classroom to participate in the video recording. Be sure to place students who did not grant permission to be video recorded in a location off-camera where they can still participate in the learning segment but not be in view of the camera.

In an instance where students without permission may have to be in the view of the camera (i.e., the classroom is very small), the TC may choose to record only the backs of the heads of those students.

While students without permission to video record are still able to participate in the classroom instruction, remember that the TC should not state their names during recording. TCs can and should include all students in the classroom activities, but for those students without permission to be video recorded, their participation should be elicited by gesturing or using eye contact.

See the edTPA handbook and *Making Good Choices* (Stanford Center for Assessment, Learning, and Equity, 2016) for further support in including students who do not have permission to be video recorded.

Last Considerations for Video Recording

As stated in the field supervisor and cooperating teacher segments (pp. 38–41 and 41–43, respectively), TCs are encouraged to practice video recording early and often before they choose the learning segment to submit for the official edTPA. If possible, record many lessons prior to the learning segment so that the camera is not a novel item in the classroom. This will provide a chance to test the equipment for sound and video quality, as well as give classroom students an opportunity to become accustomed to the camera in the room.

While the camera is recording, TCs are encouraged to teach normally and do their best to pretend the camera is not there. If the TC decides to use a camera operator, advise him or her not to interject into the lesson in any way during recording. If the TC plans to include materials on a regular or interactive whiteboard that are essential to the lesson, be sure that the video is clear. If the board is not clearly visible during the video recording, be sure to include copies of the materials in the edTPA Commentary Appendix for the reviewers.

Another aspect of the video-recording process the TC may want to consider is focusing on the students' voices, rather than their own. The video-recorded component of the edTPA submission can allow the TC the opportunity to demonstrate to the reviewers what the classroom students know and can do regarding the submitted learning segment. The TC can use the written responses to the commentaries to justify any instructional choices and fill in the blanks of what is not seen in the video segments.

On a final note, be sure to remove or cover any class- or school-identifying information while video recording. It is important to protect the confidentiality of the students and school during this process.

SUMMARY

The video-recording and analysis segment is an essential component of the edTPA. In this portion of the assessment, TCs are required to demonstrate effective teaching practices that encourage student engagement in the submitted learning segments. This chapter focused on the use of video analysis during the edTPA.

The earlier sections highlight the ways that the FS, cooperating teacher, and peers can help support the TC in the completion of the video-recording segment of the assessment. Specifically, FSs and cooperating teachers can offer TCs opportunities to practice video recording early and often, with the use of tools like graphic organizers and checklists of completion.

Outside video clips can be useful tools in preparation for the video-recording and analysis segment. Also, peers can be a valuable resource during this process. Peers can work together to critique and refine each other's teaching practices in a meaningful way during the preparation stages.

The purpose of this chapter is to empower TCs to take the lead in the video-recording and analysis process of the edTPA. Suggestions are given regarding what and when to record, how to prepare the classroom for video recording, practice use of edTPA language and prompts, and what to do with classroom students without permission to video record.

It is the hope of the authors to provide a "one-stop guide" to assist in the completion of the video recording and analysis portion of the edTPA. However, readers are advised to review all edTPA handbooks and supplemental materials for formal submission requirements.

TIPS FOR SUCCESS

The video portion of edTPA is a key element for success on this assessment. Here are a few tips for success that will help candidates:

- Video record many "practice" lessons in advance of your final recording for edTPA submission. Decide on the best position of the camera, the most optimal layout of the room, and the best position of students and yourself that show off your pedagogy.
- Use practice video experiences and camera presence to foster a relaxed atmosphere for you and your classroom students.
- Allow your peers, field supervisor, and cooperating teacher to view and critique these practice lessons. Together, you can understand and practice writing responses to edTPA prompts.
- When planning your learning segment to video record, employ effective classroom management techniques to ensure optimum student engagement.
- Demonstrate the use of appropriate academic language during the video recording.

- Provide a transcript of any portions of the video that are not audible.
- Read and understand each prompt and each rubric in the associated edTPA task.
- Crop and clip videos to the appropriate length for final submission.

REFERENCES

Kleinknecht, M., & Groschner, A. (2016). Fostering preservice teachers' noticing with structured video feedback: Results of an online- and video-based intervention study. *Teaching and Teacher Education, 59*, 45–56.

Rich, P. J., & Hannafin, M. J. (2008). Decisions and reasons: Examining preservice teacher decision-making through video self-analysis. *Journal of Computing in Higher Education, 20*(1), 62–94.

Santagata, R., & Angelici, G. (2010). Studying the impact of the lesson analysis framework on preservice teachers' abilities to reflect on videos of classroom teaching. *Journal of Teacher Education, 61*(4), 339–349.

Santagata, R., & Guarino, J. (2011). Using video to teach future teachers to learn from teaching. *Mathematics Education, 43*, 133–145.

Stanford Center for Assessment, Learning, and Equity. (2016). Making good choices: A support guide for edTPA candidates. Board of Trustees of the Leland Stanford Junior University. Retrieved from https://www.edtpa.com/Content/Docs/edTPAMGC.pdf.

Star, J. R., & Strickland, S. K. (2008). Learning to observe: Using video to improve preservice mathematics teachers' ability to notice. *Journal of Teacher Education, 11*, 107–125.

4

Technologies for Creating a Demonstration Teaching Video

PEI-LIN WENG

This chapter provides an overview of current, accessible technologies that preservice and in-service teachers can utilize for video recording. It walks readers through four basic components for creating an authentic teaching video: preparation before recording, recording, editing, and uploading. The chapter also offers a checklist to assist teachers with preparation. Finally, the author demonstrates how to follow a flowchart in a step-by-step manner to create, edit, and upload videos to a website (e.g., the edTPA website).

Video recording that captures teaching and learning activities has been a useful tool for research, evaluation, and self-reflection. Video recording can increase the authenticity of teaching and learning interactions by minimizing factors that typically exist in live observations—such as the stress of being observed or students being distracted by unfamiliar observers.

Also, video allows observers to analyze or assess activities without being physically present. It can also be viewed multiple times by multiple observers. With current technology, video can also be stored in a cloud system and be viewed by multiple users at the same time. This makes video recording more cost-effective and can save money previously required for personnel transportation and/or video product shipping.

Video recordings can also be used for self-reflection and provide many additional advantages that other self-selection tools (e.g., questionnaires) cannot offer. For example, the teacher can observe how he or she interacts with students, as well as how each student responds to the instruction.

In this chapter, we are going to focus on the "how" of video recording: how to create video *authentically* and *efficiently* for teacher candidates and their instructors. We would like to create video that authentically represents the candidates' work without being compromised by the quality of the video, such as unclear audio or video, or shaky video. In addition, we would like to help make video recording an easy process so teacher candidates can focus on instruction and not worry about the technical aspects.

The equipment and applications or software programs introduced in this chapter are, in most cases, financially practical and commercially accessible for schools and/or teacher candidates. This chapter is for a broader audience of people who want to create teaching videos for assessment purposes, but it is not limited to those who are creating teaching videos for licensure purposes (e.g., edTPA).

PREPARATION

In light of the need to protect the privacy and autonomy of students, teacher candidates must get permission from the students and their guardians before they videotape the students. Be prepared. Getting permission could be the most time-consuming and complicated process among all the tasks involved in this project (see figure 4.1). At times, it can take up to a semester. There are two things to remember: prepare this step as early as possible and don't try to do this alone. Ask for help.

After you obtain verbal agreement from the head teacher, you need to gain formal permission from the school district, which could include the school superintendents or principals. Please be aware that, for some schools, the board's permission is also required. If this is the case, you need to contact superintendents regarding this request. Superintendents will indicate if permission is granted at the school board meetings, which are held only once or twice per semester in some districts.

Once you have gained permission from the superintendents, you will also need to contact school principals to gain written permission before distributing video-recording permission forms to the students. Forms can be created by the school of teacher candidates or school districts.

Obtaining permission is sometimes an uphill battle. Here are some of the hurdles you may encounter, and how to solve them:

- Situation 1: Parents and students' unwillingness to sign the permission form

In this case, you cannot force parents or students to sign the form. As an alternative, you could record the video in such a way that it does not show the students. You could position the camera so that the unpermitted students will not be recorded. You could also use editing after the fact, such as blurring or obscuring faces, to make the students unidentifiable (Note: Check if this is acceptable to school districts or assessment requirements). This is discussed further later in this chapter.

- Situation 2: Parents not responding

There can be many reasons why you do to not get a response from the parents or guardian. They may work multiple jobs or had to travel

FIGURE 4.1
Steps required to gain permission, retrieved from Morgridge College of Education (n.d.)
Source: Pei-Lin Weng

Video/Audio Permission Form – Clinical Intern in the Classroom

Dear Parent/Guardian (or student at least 18 years old):

Your student may have a clinical intern (student teacher) in their classroom this year who is required to complete the edTPA, a state-approved performance assessment administered and overseen by Pearson Assessments in conjunction with the clinical intern's undergraduate program. The edTPA assessment is part of the process to gain initial certification as a public school teacher. It is designed to ensure that new teachers not only understand educational theory and subject matter content, but can demonstrate their ability to lead a classroom and ensure that students with diverse strengths and needs are learning. More information on the edTPA can be found on their website: http://edtpa.aacte.org and detailed information about edTPA security and privacy policies can be found here: http://www.edtpa.com/Content/Docs/ConfidentialityAndSecurity.pdf.

As part of the edTPA performance assessment, a clinical intern must demonstrate teaching effectiveness by submitting a portfolio of lessons they planned, video/audio recordings of a classroom lesson and samples of student work they have graded. Some of these materials will be shared with trained reviewers from Pearson Assessments and may also be used to train other clinical interns, faculty, and staff. These materials will be viewed under secure, password-protected conditions, never posted on publicly accessible websites. While the clinical interns are instructed not to mention students by full name in their video/audio submissions, students may appear in the video or their voices may be heard during the course of the fifteen minute presentation. Additionally, the samples of graded work submitted as part of the clinical intern's portfolio will not include any students' names or other identifying information.

Please complete the form below to indicate whether or not you grant permission for your child's participation in these activities. Thank you for your consideration and for your support as the state seeks to provide every child in New Jersey with qualified and effective educators.

Student Permission Slip edTPA Teacher Certification Assessment Tasks Please Complete and Return to your Child's Teacher on or before _____ (date)	
Student's Name:	Student's Date of Birth:
Street Address:	School:
City/State/Zip Code:	Teacher:
I am the parent/legal guardian of the child names above. I have received and read the letter regarding a teacher assessment and agree to the following: (Please initial beside either I DO or I DO NOT box below.) Your child will not be penalized if you choose: I DO NOT give permission.	
	I DO give permission to include my child's image on video recordings as he or she participates in class conducted at my child's and/or to reproduce materials that my child completed as part of the classroom activities. No student's name will appear on any materials submitted by the student teacher
	I DO NOT give permission to video record my child or reproduce materials that my child completed as part of classroom activities.
Parent/Guardian Signature:	Date:

FIGURE 4.2

Sample video permission form, New Jersey State Government

Source: Pei-Lin Weng

out of town. Some parents may not be able to read or write English and are unable to give written permission. Cooperating teachers, those most familiar with the students and their personal circumstances, can usually provide this information. If the parents are generally unavailable, you could ask the cooperating teachers to help you reach the parents and remind them to read and accept or reject the permission request.

It is recommended that the form be written at a sixth- to eighth-grade reading level so it can be read by a variety of readers. If needed, you should prepare the permission form in other languages. You can use the video permission form created by your own institution. Local districts sometimes prefer or require you to use their own video permission form. Do not forget to ask your instructors or field experience supervisor, as well as cooperating teachers, for more information and help.

Here is a resource with video-recording permission forms and letters created by William Paterson University of New Jersey, Office of Field Experience. Keep in mind that these were designed with the laws and requirements specific to the state of New Jersey and are meant only as samples: http://www.wpunj.edu/coe/departments/field/edtpa/video-recording-permissions-and-letters.

RECORDING

Teacher candidates must decide on three key elements *before* video recording:

1. What recording device to use (e.g., type of device, shooting orientation)
2. What accessories might help facilitate recording or increase video quality (e.g., tripods, microphones, stabilizers)
3. What environmental concerns must be addressed (i.e., how to set up the recording environment, position of the device, subject being recorded)

We will discuss these elements in detail.

In light of the advancements in technology, teacher candidates are faced with a choice of many different recording devices. Based on the Pew Research Center's surveys on ownership of technology devices, 86 percent of young adults now own a smartphone, and 78 percent of young adults own a computer (Smith, 2017).

Even if a teacher candidate does not own a recording device, most universities offer device-lending services to students and staff. For the purposes of this chapter, we will focus primarily on commonly seen and easily operated recording devices, discussing the advantages and disadvantages of each.

For teacher assessments, we suggest taking the video from a third-person perspective, rather than from a first-person perspective, as is commonly the case when using an action camera. This enables the viewer to observe such things as the teacher's mannerisms and body language that can be as important in communication as the spoken word.

Camera and Camcorder

Despite their primary purposes, both digital cameras and camcorders can be used for both taking still pictures and recording videos. One critical difference is that some cameras have video-recording limits (e.g., continuous 12-, 20-, 30-, and 45-minute intervals). This means that each video recording will automatically stop once preestablished time limits are reached. Teacher candidates must be cognizant of this potential complication when selecting a device.

Certain third-party software programs, such as Magic Lantern, can address this issue, but the process is often complicated. In addition, the price of cameras or video recorders varies from a modest sum to thousands of dollars. For assessment purposes, a camcorder in the price range of $100–$200 should suffice. To enable storage and transfer, cable or memory cards can be used. Many newer models also provide file transfer features via Wi-Fi.

Smartphones/Mobile Devices

Newer smartphones are often equipped with two cameras: a front camera and a rear camera. The front camera is mostly used to take "self-ies" or engage in video chats. The rear camera is used for taking most other pictures. We recommend using the rear cameras, as they offer better resolution than front cameras, typically 4–14 megapixels (MP) as opposed to 1.2–2 MP with the front camera.

Laptop

Most laptops are equipped with a built-in camera and can be used to create videos. The resolution of laptop cameras varies. We cannot simply judge the resolution according to the year of the model. For example, a 2016 MacBook (12 inches) houses a 480p FaceTime camera, while a 2012 MacBook Air (11 inches) is equipped with a 720p Face-Time camera.

Because of its low resolution, the 480p camera is not recommended for recording teaching assessment videos. We suggest using at least a 720p camera which provides 1280 × 720 pixels (i.e., 921,600 pixels or 0.9 MP). If a laptop does not have a built-in camera, a webcam can be added at a cost of approximately $20, and up.

Action Cameras

One type of video-recording device that has gained popularity in recent years is the lightweight action camera. There are several on the market now, such as the Spy Tec Mobius, Activeon CX Gold, Solo Lega-zone, and the popular GoPro. GoPro, for example, has several different models such as the Hero5 Black (44.5 × 62 × 32 mm, touch screen) and the Hero5 Session (38 × 38 × 36 mm; no touch screen). You can record video continuously for 1.5–2.5 hours.

GoPro provides three fields of view, or FOV, referring to the amount of the scene that the camera can capture: Ultrawide: 170-degree FOV, Medium: 127-degree FOV, and Narrow: 90-degree FOV. Users can select the most appropriate FOV based on their classroom setup.

There are many ways to access GoPro videos. You can live-stream, upload automatically to the cloud, or transfer files directly from the camera or the camera's SD card.

Another extra portable camera is the Polaroid Cube+. It is a cube-shaped camera measuring 35 × 35 ×35 mm, with a magnetic base that will attach to any metal surface, such as a metal cabinet in a classroom. It can record up to 90 minutes of video clips per charge. The Polaroid Cube ranges in price from $50 to $199. However, reviewers have raised concerns regarding its audio quality. Like the GoPro Hero Session, the Polaroid Cube has no LCD preview on the device. However, you can stream via Wi-Fi to your mobile devices.

For more details on the specifications and features of different types of recording devices, visit this interactive website: https://www.productchart.com. For a side-by-side comparison, simply highlight the brands of interest and then compare.

Accessories: Microphone

Audio quality is an important component of a video clip. It provides critical information for the reviewer to assess teaching. If the recording device is far away from the speaker, the audio is likely to be compromised by the noises of a natural environment.

There are many methods to increase the audio quality of the video recording, including separately recording the audio (which requires editing software to combine audio and video) or using an external microphone. We suggest the latter approach, because it does not require additional editing, which is not allowed for assessment-based video.

Before recording, it is critical to be aware of the naturally occurring ambient sound in the camera's location. Classrooms are dynamic environments with many unavoidable noise sources, from HVAC air handlers to pencil sharpeners. Therefore, we recommend using an external microphone, especially for devices such as smartphones or action cameras, to achieve sharper audio quality, even if the classroom has high ambient noise levels.

There are many different types of external microphones, such as wired, on-device, and wireless microphones. However, for recording teaching activities, we typically place the video devices far away from the voice source (i.e., teacher candidates). Therefore, we recommend using a wireless microphone, as described here for the iPhone and GoPro cameras.

For the iPhone, you will need a wireless lavalier microphone (a small clip-on microphone, for example, Sennheiser EW 112P or Sony ECMAW4 Wireless Microphone) and an adaptor to connect the microphone receiver to headphones. For more information, go to these YouTube clips: https://www.youtube.com/watch?v=VrbXAS2aosY&t=343s and https://www.youtube.com/watch?v=00pn9r2wJ8w.

There is a simple product designed for the GoPro camera. It is a Bluetooth microphone (Removu M1) and a receiver (Removu A1) that can directly clip onto a GoPro device.

Accessories: Tripod

A tripod can anchor the recording device to an appropriate angle and height, and provide stability (very important!) for better video quality. It can be placed on the floor or a table, and record the scene without being obstructed by classroom objects or surrounding students.

There are two things to consider when selecting a tripod: good balance between the tripod head and the recording device to prevent tipping, and appropriate mounts connecting your recording device to a quick-release plate on the tripod.

Besides the traditional tripod (which can extend up to 72 inches), there are other options available for more lightweight video-recording devices. You need to pay attention to the recommended maximum load weight for the tripod.

If you have a surface available, such as a desk, on which to place a tripod, you can choose from some of the following types of supports.

- Mini tripod: The RetiCAM extends to a maximum height of 19 inches and can handle cameras weighing up to 6 lbs., or AmazonBasics with a maximum extension of 7.5 inches and a maximum load rating of 1.1 lbs.
- Octopus tripod: (e.g., JOBY GorillaPod, with a maximum load rating of 6.6 lbs.)—The Octopus-style tripod can stand alone on a surface or be wrapped around a chair or a rod.
- Selfie stick, with a tripod stand: The benefit of this tripod is that the stick can be extended to more than 45 inches. One drawback is that this type of tripod is not as stable as others when fully extended. Also, note that not all selfie sticks have the tripod function.

Accessories: Wide-Angle lenses

Those who use smartphones to record video may have noticed that video images were cropped 20–40 percent as compared to the still pictures taken using the same smartphone camera. If you would like to capture more classroom items or students in the scene, you can add an accessory called a *wide-angle lens* to your smartphone. There is a wide array of add-on lenses for smartphones found on many web-popular sites, such as Amazon, with prices ranging from around $10 to as much as you would care to spend.

Accessories: Stabilizer

Watching a shaky video can be uncomfortable and can make it difficult for viewers to focus on what is happening in the clip. The use of a tripod in a regular classroom setting is recommended, instead of asking a third person to hold the recording device (with or without a built-in stabilizer).

However, a third person may be needed to hold the recording device in some situations, such as recording an outdoor class activity. In some situations, you may still be able to use a tripod; however, for most outdoor recordings, we recommend using a stabilizer when possible. Examples include the DJI Osmo mobile for iPhone ($299) and the Sutefoto Handheld Stabilizer Pro Version for Camera ($61.99).

Testing before Recording

Long before recording begins, it's important for teacher-videographers to fully understand how all of their devices will work together. Carefully explore compatibility between devices, software, and websites before recording. It can be time-consuming and frustrating to discover, after you have recorded your video, that it cannot be directly read or edited by a certain computer software program or by the website to which you intend to upload.

Although there are software programs that will convert video formats, not everyone has the necessary knowledge to effectively operate the software. If, however, you find you have need of one, there are several free applications available through the Internet, such as "Freemake Video Converter" and "Any Video Converter Free."

Other Things to Consider

- Orientation: When recording a video using a smartphone, make sure to position the smart device in a horizontal position so that it will provide a horizontally recorded video that is more ideal for viewing than a vertical one.
- Storage capacity and limits: Before you begin recording, make sure you have enough storage space. The storage capacity will be affected by the resolution settings you choose. For example, increasing the resolution will increase the size of the video.
- How to change resolutions on an iPhone: Click on the "Setting" icon and select, "Photos & Camera." On the lower left of the screen, click on "Record Video." A dialog box will appear with a choice of 720p HD at 30 fps, 1080p HD at 30 fps, or 1080p at 60 fps. The higher pixel rate (1080p) produces a larger, clearer image. The most commonly used fps, or frames-per-second rate, for video recording is 30 fps; 60 fps would be best suited to fast-action video recording, doubling the usual number of individual frames per second while producing a series of still images with less blurring of movement, but requiring at least twice as much memory. For most teaching videos, the 720p/30 fps option is sufficient.

Resolutions	1 minute	1 hour
720p HD at 30 fps	60 MB	3.5 GB
1080p HD at 30 fps	130 MB	7.6 GB
1080p HD at 60 fps	200 MB	11.7 GB
4K HD	375 MB	21.9 GB

FIGURE 4.3
Adapted from Costello (2017), How Much Video Can You Record on an iPhone?
Source: Pei-Lin Weng

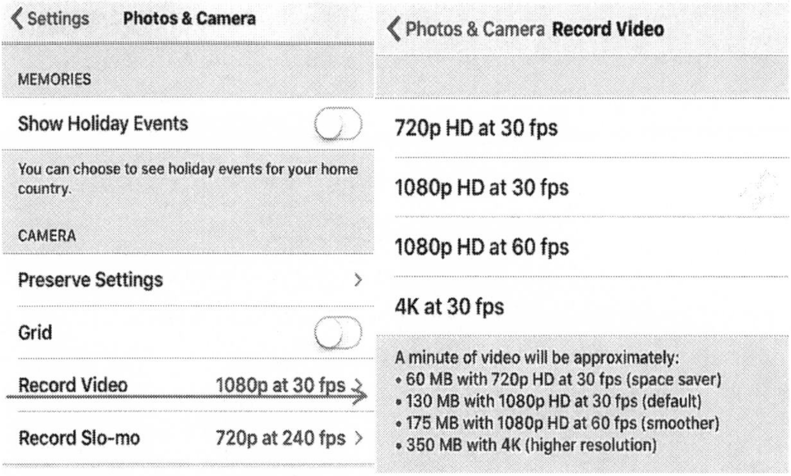

FIGURE 4.4
Changing iPhone video resolution
Source: Pei-Lin Weng

- Environment (e.g., lighting, arrangement): It is recommended that the recording device be placed between the light source (e.g., light coming in through windows) and the target teachers or students. Situations where the target teachers and students are positioned between the light source and the recording device should be avoided.

- Duration: Record the teaching activities for as long as you can.
- Backup equipment: Like a wedding photographer, it is important for you to have backup equipment for this "once-in-a-lifetime" event.

Other Useful Links

1. Recommended video formats and settings: https://www.edtpa.com/ Content/Docs/RecommendedVideoFormatsandSettings.pdf.
2. iPhone's video resolutions and storage space: https://www.lifewire. com/how-much-video-can-iphone-record-2000304.

EDITING

Editing should be limited in order to present authentic teaching activities. Here are some acceptable reasons for editing an assessment-based video:

(a) Trimming the beginning and the end of the video from a longer clip
(b) Dividing an originally long video clip into smaller clips to upload (due to size limitations)

FIGURE 4.5
An example of how to divide a video using Apple's iMovie app
Source: Pei-Lin Weng

(c) Combining video clips that were divided into several clips due to size limits for uploading or that were divided due to the recording device's batteries running out or a memory card's storage space limitations

(d) Compressing video clips to decrease the size for uploading due to upload size limitations (e.g., Video Compressor app)

(e) Converting an invalid video file to an appropriate format for upload. Recommended video format types include the following: .avi (Audio Visual Interleave), .mov (QuickTime Movie), .mp4 (Moving Pictures Expert Group 4), and .wmv (Windows Media Video). For a licensure website (e.g., edTPA), approved formats include the following: .asf, .avi, .flv, .m4v, .mp4, .mov, .mpeg, .mpg, .qt, and .wmv. (This information is based on the edTAP website.)

(f) Adding captions: If the student's voice is not clear, you can add text to the video using either iMovie or Windows Movie Maker. Make sure you transcribe speech faithfully. Do not guess, add, or alter what has been said.

(g) Concealing a person's, especially a student's, identity: If the person whose identity needs to be concealed is not moving around in the video, you can use iMovie or Windows Movie Maker to "block" the target person's face. To do so, simply add an overlay image to video footage and block the target person's face. However, this works only if the movement of the target person is limited.

If the person in question is moving around, you will need to use a more advanced software program or application. One of the more popular pieces of software for this purpose is Adobe Premiere Pro CC, which is available on a subscription basis from Adobe at a cost of $19.99 per month for teachers and students.

For further information on how to mask a moving figure, visit these two websites: https://helpx.adobe.com/uk/premiere-pro/how-to/blur-face-masking-tracking.html and http://tutvid.com/video-editing/blur-moving-faces-distort-audio-hide-identity-premiere-pro-tutorial/.

UPLOADING

Once the video is in its final form, has been formatted and edited, and is ready for viewing, the final step is storage of the video for future reference. In most cases this will involve uploading the video to a cloud service, online video service, or, in the case of teacher candidates submitting for licensure purposes, to an accrediting service such as edTPA.

Cloud Storage

You can upload videos from your laptop or desktop computer, a website, a smartphone, or tablet. Candidates need to be aware of the upload size limitation. For emails servers, upload limits are usually capped at around 20–25 MB. For cloud services such as iCloud, Google Drive, and Dropbox, the upload limits are based on your remaining storage space.

Online Video

For Edmodo, an educational website, the upload limit is 100 MB. For YouTube, the upload limit is 128 GB after you verify your contact number. Without verifying your contact number, you can upload a video of only 15 minutes or less. Vimeo, another popular website for hosting and sharing videos, allows uploads of as much as 500 MB per week, under the free plan.

edTPA Video

Accreditation by edTPA is, in many states, a critical requirement for working as a teacher today. Part of the application for this licensure involves teacher assessment videos. This portion of the chapter will help in getting the video uploaded to edTPA for consideration. One of the first considerations is the size of the video being submitted. Two things will have a direct effect on the file's size: the format used and the fact that the video must be a continuous, linear recording with no deletions or section edits.

If the video was recorded at high resolution and lasts an hour or more, it is probably not going to fit within the 500-MB file size limit set by edTPA. Since edTPA requires that the video must be a continuous recording without interruption or edits, a file that is too large cannot simply be trimmed down to size by removing irrelevant or repetitious portions.

However, data compression may be able to reduce the file size enough to squeeze it into something less than 500 MB. There are free software tools available for this purpose, listed in the edTPA website FAQs. They are http://www.any-video-converter.com/products/for_video_free/ (for Windows PCs) and https://itunes.apple.com/us/app/any-video-converter-lite/id479472944 (for Mac).

It should be noted that the 500-MB size restriction applies only to *individual* files being uploaded to edTPA. There is *no* upload limit to the *entire* candidate's submission.

Because most teacher candidate videos will probably be assembled, formatted, cropped, and otherwise made ready for uploading to edTPA using either a Mac or a Windows computer, we will look at the upload procedures for only three software applications: iMovie 9.0.9 and iPhoto 9.6.1 for Mac users, and Windows Movie Maker (2012 version). Thanks to similarities in most task-specific software applications, these examples may still prove helpful in many less ubiquitous operating systems (Textbox 4.1).

First, let's look at the Apple Mac iMovie 9.0.9 upload process. If you are working on a Mac and don't have iMovie version 9.0.9, you will find a free download of that version at http://support.apple.com/kb/dl1574. Open iMovie, create a new blank project from the File menu. Don't add any effects. If your video clip is not displayed in your Event Library, select "Import" from the File menu and navigate to "Movies" where you should find your video.

Click on your video (choosing "Select Entire Clip" in the Edit menu) and click the button marked "Add selected video to Project." Now, in the "Share" menu, click on "Export Movie." You will be asked for the size to export. Choose "Mobile," navigate to your desktop, and click the "Export" button. Wait a bit, while your video is compressed and exported, and then log into your portfolio on the edTPA website and upload the video from your desktop. Your video is now part of your portfolio.

If you've been using iPhoto on your Mac, the upload instructions are even simpler than with iMovie. If you do not have version 9.6.1, you can update through the Mac App Store. Your video will already be listed in your iPhoto Library. Simply go to the Library and select your video. When selected, it will display a yellow border. Be sure you have selected only the one correct video clip, then choose "Export" from the File menu.

In the "File Export" tab, indicate "Kind" as "Original." Then click "Export" and save the file on your desktop. From this point on, the process is the same as discussed earlier, with iMovie: log onto your edTPA portfolio and upload the video from your desktop. Remember, if your file size is too large and seems to be taking too long to upload, consider using one of the free video compression applications mentioned earlier. It is usually a good idea to compress files larger than 300 MB.

Finally, this is the process to follow using Windows Movie Maker to add a video to your edTPA portfolio. If your PC doesn't already have Windows Movie Maker 2012 installed, go to http://windows.microsoft. com/en-us/windows/get-movie=maker-download. Follow the website's and the installer's instructions.

Mac and Windows flowcharts: preparation steps for edTPA video upload

iMovie: File→New Project→Event Library→Your Video→Edit→Select Entire Clip→Add to Project→Export Movie→Share→Size to Export→ Mobile→Export. Upload.

iPhoto: iPhoto Library→Your Movie→File→Export→Kind→Original→ Export. Upload.

Windows Movie Maker: Select Video, Save Movie→Common settings→For email→MPEG-4/H,264 Video File (*.mp4)→Save. Upload.

TEXTBOX 4.1
Source: Pei-Lin Weng

	Check Box	Note:
PREPARATION		
Agreement from classroom teachers		
Permission from superintendent and/or principal		
Gaining consent from parents and students		
Make appointment with classroom teachers to visit the classroom (preparing for recording)		
RECORDING EQUIPMENT		
Video recording device (e.g., digital camcorder, digital camera, smartphone, mobile device, computer)		
Backup recording device		
Accessories (e.g., tripod, microphone, wide-angle lenses, stabilizer if needed)		
RECORDING ENVIRONMENT/ARRANGEMENT		
Location (e.g., classroom, auditorium, outdoor)		
Students' seating arrangement*		
Device placement**		
Dry run		
VIDEO SPECIFICATIONS		
Duration		
Size		
File formats		
Resolution		
Compatibility with uploading editing software programs and websites		
EDITING		
Editing device		
Editing software/applications***		
UPLOADING AND STORING		
Designated place		
Storage place		

*To avoid recording students who do not give consent for recording.
**Make sure you consider the sounds, lighting, and other background factors)
***Based on the modality to be added (e.g., adding captions, concealing identity of subjects)

FIGURE 4.6

Comprehensive preparation checklist

Source: Pei-Lin Weng

Open Windows Movie Maker, select your video, and choose "Save movie" in the top right corner. Be sure to click on the text, not the icon, to access the menu. In the menu, go to "Common settings" and choose "For email." In the next window, choose to save your video as "MPEG-4/H.264 Video File (*.MP4)"; go back to your desktop and click "Save."

There will be a little wait while your video is compressed and exported, but when done you need only to log into your edTPA portfolio, online, and upload your video from your desktop.

SUMMARY

In this chapter, we have looked at and discussed a broad selection of the current technologies that are accessible to both preservice and in-service teachers for video-recording classroom lessons, both for the creation of authentic teaching videos and for the documentation of teacher candidates' pedagogical skills for licensure purposes.

After examining the details of preparing to record these videos, the actual recording process, and some editing considerations, we've concluded the chapter with a detailed documentation of the steps required to upload the video to the cloud or edTPA, including a comprehensive checklist, and a "day before official recording" checklist. It is hoped that this book may demystify some of the more technical areas of the subject matter, enabling teachers to enjoy the benefits of video recording in the service of education.

BEFORE VIDEO RECORDING

        Confirm date/time/location with the head teacher
        Recording device: charge battery
        Recording device: check settings
        Recording device: check space on the memory card or device
        Bring backup recording devices
        Bring necessary accessories (see the checklist)
        Set up environment
        Record a short video (e.g., 10 seconds) on site and check
                the background, sounds, lighting, stability, etc.

FIGURE 4.7
The "Day-before" checklist
Source: Pei-Lin Weng

REFERENCES

Costello, S. (2017). How much video can you record on an iPhone? *Lifewire*. Retrieved from https://www.lifewire.com/how-much-video-can-iphone-record-2000304

Morgridge College of Education (n.d.). *Procedures/checklist for recording video and audio in pre K-12 schools and classrooms*. Retrieved from http://morgridge.du.edu/wp-content/uploads/2014/04/Procedures-for-Recording-Video-in-K12-Classrooms.pdf

Smith, A. (2017). Record shares of Americans now own smartphones, have home broadband. *Pew Research Center*. Retrieved from http://www.pewresearch.org/fact-tank/2017/01/12/evolution-of-technology/

Index

Note: page numbers in italics indicate tables.

73

About the Editors

Carrie Eunyoung Hong, Ph.D., is associate professor of literacy at William Paterson University of New Jersey. She is directing the Masters of Education in Literacy program in which classroom teachers are trained to be certified reading specialists. She has extensive experience directing federal and state grant programs that provide teacher professional development. Her research interests include reading, writing, balanced literacy, literacy teacher education, and teacher preparation to work with culturally and linguistically diverse learners. She is the author of refereed articles and book chapters in the area of teacher education and professional development.

Irene Van Riper, Ed.D., has in-depth experience and expertise as a teacher educator, consultant, researcher, and author in all levels of education from early childhood and middle school to higher education as a professor of special education. Her work has led her to specialize in autism spectrum disorder, dyslexia, and the preparation of teachers for understanding students with disabilities. She was instrumental in developing a graduate program in autism education and has earned associate-level certification from the Academy of Orton-Gillingham Practitioners and Educators. She is the author of peer-reviewed articles and editor of a book in the areas of teacher preparation and special education.

About the Contributors

Robert Cooper is director of the Jump Start Program at Manhattanville College. Jump Start is an accelerated teacher certification program providing an alternative pathway to New York State certification for second career candidates. During Mr. Cooper's 20 years in the New York City public schools, he served as a high school English teacher and assistant principal. Upon his move to Westchester County, he served for 14 years as the English department chair and assistant superintendent in the Bedford Central School District. He has extensive experience in teacher induction, staff development, and teacher/administrator evaluation.

Stephen J. Hernandez, Ed.D., is associate dean for Grants and Teacher Performance Assessment at Hofstra University on Long Island, New York, where he coordinates student preparation for the edTPA teacher certification assessment in the School of Education. He is also director of Early Childhood Special Education and serves as adjunct professor in the Special Education. In addition to Dr. Hernandez's work in academia, he has worked for over 40 years serving children with special needs and their families in community-based settings. Dr. Hernandez has held positions ranging in scope from direct care service provider to classroom instructor to over 22 years in various educational leadership positions in the New York metropolitan area. Dr. Hernandez earned his B.A. from

Fordham University, an M.S. in education from Long Island University-Brooklyn College, a professional diploma in educational administration from Fordham University's Graduate School of Education, and his doctor of education from Hofstra University. His areas of research include student teacher preparation, collaborative teaming, interdisciplinary intervention, and the management of children's challenging behavior. He has been published in numerous national and international publications. Dr. Hernandez is a member of the Council for Exceptional Children, the National Association for the Education of the Young Child, The American Academy of Special Education Professionals, and The International Association of Special Education.

Nikki L. Josephs, Ph.D., is assistant professor in the Department of Special Education at Manhattanville College, where she teaches graduate-level courses in classroom management, instructional strategies, transition to post high-school life for students with disabilities, and research techniques. In addition, Dr. Josephs serves as a professional development school liaison and field supervisor at an elementary school in White Plains, New York. She maximizes the boundaries of the professional development school relationship by encouraging teamwork and community building between P-12 classroom teachers, students, and college-level teacher candidates. Her current research interests and publications focus on gender-specific programming and interventions that address the academic needs of adolescents with emotional and/or behavior disorders.

Arleen Schefflein has been adjunct professor at Lehman and Manhattanville College for six years, teaching courses on behavior management, special education, field supervision, and student teaching. She is also supervisor for Achieve Beyond, where she supervises at least 100 special education itinerant teachers and presents training workshops. She has also been adjunct at Mt. Saint Vincent, Fordham University, and California State University of Northridge. As assistant director for the Yonkers

School District and SWBOCES, she supervised many out-of-district programs. Preceding SWBOCES, she served as supervisor for special education at Warwick Valley School District and provided instruction for teachers and related service providers for elementary, middle, and high schools. She is certified as an administrator and has duel certification in social studies and special education.

Pei-Lin Weng, Ph.D., CCC-SLP, is assistant professor in the Department of Special Education and Professional Counseling at William Paterson University of New Jersey. She specializes in assistive technology, augmentative and alternative communication, and autism. Her current research focuses on video-based instruction, mathematics learning, and design features of instructional technology.

Made in the USA
San Bernardino, CA
18 June 2019